BROKEN TO BEAUTIFUL

BROKENNESS IS NOT THE END OF YOUR STORY

JEANNINE BENNETT

Published in Virginia Beach, Virginia, U.S.A. by Vision to Purpose. www.visiontopurpose.com.

Cover design by Mark W. Lambertson of ProdigiousMotion.com.
Cover photo by Jill Wellington from Pixabay.

Print: ISBN: 9781080214341
Printed in the United States of America.
First Printing August 2019

DEDICATION

I dedicate this book to my husband, Hayden, without whose constant support, encouragement, and love, this book would have been impossible to write.

And to my children Sandra, Brittany, and Zachary, who supported and loved me unconditionally through the trials and joys of my life.

And finally, to my mother for her love and support.

CONTENTS

INTRODUCTION

Have you ever agreed to do something, and right after you did, complete and utter panic set in? Well, that's what happened to me at the beginning of this year. All I could think was, why on earth did I agree to do it?

One Sunday, as I was volunteering in the children's wing at church, a friend stopped by to tell me she passed my name along as a potential speaker for a ladies' retreat. She was invited to speak at her mother's church but had a scheduling conflict, so she thought of me and gave my name to the church contact. At first, I was thrilled, especially since I had been telling my friend that I needed to line up speaking engagements to help promote my business. I launched Vision to Purpose full-time in October 2017, but up to this point, I had focused all my energy on refining my service offerings. Now I was ready to pursue new things, and engaging people face-to-face was a top priority.

On Monday, I was surprised to find an email from the church point of contact referencing the speaking engagement and asking if I would be interested in addressing the women during their annual ladies' retreat. How God Captured Your Heart was the theme of the retreat. I loved it until I realized I had no clue when God capture my heart. I reread that line of the email, could you please share with the ladies how God captured your heart? As I drifted off in thought, my mind went blank. I had nothing! Truth be told, I had never thought about how God captured my heart.

"Can you pinpoint the exact moment when God captured your heart?"

In my brain, God just did; end of story. Until that moment, I never thought about an exact point in time, I just felt my connection to God grow and get stronger. I grew comfortable in my relationship with Him, and that's all that mattered, right? That sounded good, but how on earth was I going to share that with the ladies? The engagement would be over in 2 minutes. Who could I possibly help with that conclusion? I could just see it, "Ladies, God captured my heart, yes He sure did, I don't know when, but He got it. When's lunch?" It wasn't very enlightening in my head and would be even less so in person. I knew that if I were going to address the ladies' group, I had better figure it out quickly.

I told the lady I would pray about the opportunity and

respond when I was ready. It's what we are taught to do. Seek God for discernment, for wisdom. We need time to think about it, feel comfortable with the decision before we move forward on it, right?

I wrestled with the concept for three weeks. It became overwhelming to think through the exact moment. I know that probably sounds weird, but nothing I have ever done has been traditional, and finding God wasn't either. It was not one moment in time that sealed the deal for God and me, but rather a life-long journey that did it. Remember the story of the 99 sheep the Shepherd left for the 1? I was the one, and boy, was I lost for a long time!

God revealed that's where my testimony began. The day He went in search of me because I kept going down the wrong path.

Isn't it funny how life has a way of taking us in so many directions? God has a perfect plan for us, yet for reasons unknown we choose to go our own way, ignorant of the fact that while we are straying there is no better plan than His. Is it the enemy's deceitful lies or our own selfish search for superficial happiness that causes us to stumble in a world where instant gratification is alive and well?

God did indeed capture my heart, albeit over years, so after three weeks I decided I was ready to accept the opportunity to speak at the event. Deep down I was terrified. I contacted the church, secretly hoping the lady would say "no, we already found another speaker," but no such luck. The woman was thrilled that I was available and informed me that I was going to be the main session of the day. I hung up the phone and had a minor panic attack. Main session? I thought I was going to speak during a small session, which in my mind meant at most, ten women listening to me. No, it was a main session on the stage in the sanctuary. Please understand, I love God and wanted to share His good Word, but I realized that sharing when God captured my heart meant telling a room full of strangers my entire testimony, something I had never done before.

My testimony is a series of events and reads like a combination of a tragedy, comedy, drama and horror show. It is full of hurt, deceit, grief, heartache, and devastation, but also full of great joy, many blessings, countless rewards, lots of love, and a whole bunch of never-ending hope.

How can I fit all of that in a one-hour presentation? Did I need to create a PowerPoint? I was so accustomed to creating PowerPoints. Do you show PowerPoints in the sanctuary? I was treading on uncharted territory. This was not like working for the Navy and giving a presentation to the Admiral. Trust me when I say that I had to talk myself off the ledge. "No, Jeannine, the ladies do not want to see a presentation on your life. How disturbing would that be for them to see pictures of your horror show on a big screen? You do not want to traumatize anyone; they will never want you to come back."

I stopped panicking and did the only thing I knew to do, I prayed. This was God's story too. "God, please guide me in telling our story. Please give me courage to do it and do it well. Thank you, Father!"

Praise be to God! This book is written because He did indeed give me the courage to share our story.

God works in mysterious ways and this time was no different. After I spoke that day, those same women asked if I planned to write a book detailing my life. They felt it would help others. They even suggested I reach out to my friend, the same one who passed my name along, because she is an author with more than 70 books to her name. They figured if I didn't want to write it, perhaps I could hire her to do it.

I left that retreat humbled, energized and blessed.

To fulfill the promise I made to the ladies, I did chat with my friend about my experience after the retreat and mentioned the potential of writing a book. She was thrilled. She encouraged me to share my story and gave me some wonderful suggestions to help me get started. As a result of her guidance, the remainder of this book is what was created.

Like the ladies during that retreat, I invite you on this personal journey with me. It is my desire that the unfolding of my testimony combined with God's Word will give you the strength to overcome trials and challenges of life you may be facing right now. It is also my hope that you would consider sharing your story to help others too. God has given each of us a unique purpose, which means no other person has your exact story. You are exclusively qualified to tell it.

To support you as you go on this journey with me, I want

to keep you encouraged. The stories I share are vivid. They may trigger unexpected emotions, especially if you have dealt with similar trials or are dealing with your own challenges right now. To keep us inspired and focused on God's presence, I will share three things at the end of each chapter: (1) God's Planned Outcome, (2) God's Word, and (3) Reflection Questions.

God's Planned Outcome

It has taken me a lifetime to realize that God does indeed have a plan for every one of us. He knew before we were born what our life would be. He knows the outcome of every challenge, each decision we will make, and even the desires of our heart. In going through this journey of self-reflection, I have been able to look back and see how God worked everything together for His good. Nothing I experienced was forgotten or wasted. Everything was used for His glory and my good. I will reveal what I believe to be God's outcome after every chapter to illustrate how God makes everything work together even when we do not see it while walking through it.

God's Holy Word

To offer God's planned outcomes, I must share His Word.

His plans can be found in the Holy Scripture and solidify the promises He has made to us. His Word will keep us encouraged as we travel this journey of mixed emotions together.

Questions to Reflect On

I have found that reflecting on life, although difficult at times, can yield answers to unresolved questions. To help us grow during our journey, I will pose questions after every chapter. The questions are simply to get you thinking about things you have experienced and how God has captured your heart through them.

Let's start with some examples.

God's Planned Outcome

God knew before I did that I was going to speak. God brought a church sister into my life that gave me a gentle nudge in the right direction. She presented an opportunity for me to share my story and then He gave me the courage to speak it. He even brought the right people to hear my testimony. Those ladies were chosen by God to encourage me to share this story with others.

God's Holy Word

God never said that Christians would live trouble-free. In fact, Jesus promises us that we will face tribulation. The good news is that 1) we are not alone and 2) He has a plan. Here are some verses that I read when faced with tough issues.

There is no one like the God of Jeshurun, who rides on the heavens to help you and on the clouds in his majesty. The eternal God is your refuge, and underneath are the everlasting arms. (Deuteronomy 33:26-27 NIV)

I have said these things to you, that in me you may have peace. In the world you will have tribulation. But take heart; I have overcome the world. (John 16:33 ESV)

And we know that in all things God works for the good of those who love him, who have been called according to his purpose. (Romans 8:28 ESV)

Questions to Reflect On

A journal is a great place to respond to the following questions. If you don't feel like you are facing any challenges right now, you can jot down the joy you feel in this season of blessing.

1. Are you going through a challenge in life right now?

2. Are you trusting God in the process as you deal with that challenge or are you trying to drive the outcome?

3. Do you think you will ever be able to share your testimony? If not, what is holding you back from doing so? If it is fear, what are you afraid of?

I

BROKEN

CREATED ON PURPOSE

There I stood on stage with everyone looking at me. "Okay, God, You say You never leave me so I am trusting your Word. I sure could use some of that courage You gave David about now."

I placed my Bible and speaker notes on the podium, took a deep breath, and looked around. It felt a bit strange being on the sanctuary stage looking out at a crowd of attendees instead of being in the pews with everyone else.

I asked the ladies to pray with me because the journey I was about to take them on was going to be a bit bumpy. I am not sure they understood what I meant or what they were going to hear that day, but they obliged. We prayed and I began.

"Who in here has seen a Lifetime movie?" Of course, every hand went up. "Good, then you are about to hear something that will resonate with what you have seen on television!"

"Discovering how God captured my heart was a long road and came in the form of life reflection after moving past tragedy, trials, and pain to see blessings. To help you understand what I mean, I need to share my testimony in its entirety, but I promise I won't go past my hour timeframe. At least I hope not."

Here is my testimony as shared that day.

I grew up in an abusive home where yelling was a common occurrence. I didn't go to church unless I was visiting grandparents. Both sets of grandparents were Catholic. My step grandmother was Hispanic, so I experienced church in both Spanish and English. My paternal grandmother was French, but church in upper Michigan was always in English. Both types of services had commonality though I never quite understood some of the traditions. For instance, why did we have to stand, sit, kneel, stand, sit, kneel and stand, sit, kneel so many times during the service? I also didn't get why we had to make a cross on our bodies. My Spanish grandmother always added an extra touch by blowing a kiss to God after the crossing ritual. I thought that was kind of cool, so I mimicked her actions as I was learning. My French grandmother, a bit more conservative, did not appreciate the added gesture. I received the look--you know the one, that long confident stare where the person giving it never blinks. Yes, that was my grandmother's way of telling me to knock it off.

My first real encounter with God (or so I thought) was after I accidentally opened the Bible to the book of Revelations when I was about six. I am going to admit right here and now that reading about the end of times at such a young age started a long-time fear of God. Can you imagine what reading words such as death, fire, and brimstone meant to a little one? I remember dropping the Bible, afraid of what I read. I put that Bible back on the shelf and for years, every time I walked by that shelf, I would glance over to make sure it was still securely stowed away so as not to come out to get me.

I have always known God existed, even before going to church and reading portions of Revelations. I guess that demonstrates God is the only one who can fill a void in our beings. He truly desires relationship with us. I didn't know much, but at some point, I concluded that I needed to be good or God would be disappointed and punish me. I have often thought that perhaps my parents used God as a threat to get me to behave, but that couldn't be; we did not go to church or use God's name except when cursing. My mom was the most vocal and short tempered with me. I never wanted to make her mad.

Today, I realize that there were some very good reasons for the way my mom acted when I was younger. She had no mother figure growing up. In my 30s, I discovered my mom's mom, my Grandma Charlotte, had three children by the time she was 25. My guess is she was unhappy in her marriage and seeking a divorce. I believe she already found a new boyfriend and spent much of her time hanging out with him at the bar. In the 1950s it was customary for the mother to get the children in a divorce; however, it is my belief my grandmother did not want her children. She was enjoying her newfound single life too much. Since my grandmother did not want her kids and this was the 1950s, the only option was for the courts to place my mom and her siblings in an orphanage until they could determine if the father was capable of caring for them. I am not sure how long my mom and her siblings stayed there, but I remember my mother saying that it seemed like months before matters were handled. At five years old, my mother cared for her little brother and sister, trying to hold the family together. To this day, I believe my almost 70-year-old mother still struggles with feelings of abandonment.

My mom grew up too fast and had no mother to guide her; I think she got pregnant at 13 years old. Having daughters of my own and now granddaughters, I can't imagine them pregnant at such an innocent age.

As an unwed mother with no parental support, I believe my mother was forced to live underground in the basement of a church hidden away from the rest of the world. The church connected to a hospital through a tunnel. This arrangement was used for all unwed teen mothers so as not to be an embarrassment to their parents or society. I imagine there were plenty of young girls in her same situation. Many of them were rebellious. She shared stories of girls escaping through a window on several occasions to see their boyfriends (the baby's father). I am still baffled as to how as a pregnant girl they could fit through a small window or have enough energy to run all over town to see their boyfriends.

I remember being pregnant with my son, Zachary. I had gained 50 pounds during my pregnancy, and about 49 of those pounds were belly. One day after work, I went to the parking lot to get in my car and drive home. I discovered two large SUVs blocked me in on both sides. Looking at my belly and then back at the space between cars I knew there was no way I was going to enter through the driver's side or passenger side of my car. I cried!

Have you ever broken down because you thought a situation was hopeless? I sobbed for a while until I realized I was never going to get home if I didn't figure out what to do. Turns out the only way to get in the SUV was popping the back and climbing in. Not so bad, until it was time to climb over the back seat and then into the driver's seat past the gear shift. It was a close call at times, but praise God, I managed. I laugh about the ordeal now. How funny I must have looked, eight months pregnant doing gymnastic maneuvering in the back of my car.

So, picturing anyone squeezing through a window was a bit hilarious. Funny how there is nothing that will deter us when we think we are in love. Have you ever done anything because you were blinded by love? I know I have!

Since my Grandma Charlotte would not help, I believe my mother was forced to give her child over to the state for adoption. I also believe my mother gave birth to a beautiful baby boy. It is customary to hold a child a few minutes after birth and again right before signing the adoption paperwork. Once the paperwork is signed, girls never see their children again.

At the age of 16 I believe my mom married Dan, the baby's father. Together they tried to find their son but the records were sealed and without parental rights no one would help them. Shortly thereafter, my mother had another child, my sister Tammy, whom I did not know existed until I was a teenager, when I overheard my aunts discussing the fact secretly in another room.

I didn't get to meet Tammy until I was 40 years old. It was funny to think Pammy, Danny and Tammy. Perhaps my mom had a little sense of humor--something I didn't see until I was in my 30s.

My mom's first marriage did not last long; I think she was divorced by the age of 18. She was forced to get a job but struggled because her options were limited but having a well-developed body opened the door to a job as a go-go dancer.

Of course, being a stripper was not the best environment for a child, so I guess she arranged for her ex-mother-in-law to care for Tammy until she could find a better job and safer place to live. Even with a job, saving enough money must have proved difficult, so I assume she chose to leave Tammy with her ex-mother in law to raise.

A year later, she met my dad and planned to have a baby (me). It appeared that she felt such love from my dad's family and wanted to be a part of something she never had before. I believe mom had dreams of moving from Wisconsin, to Michigan, but my dad had no desire to move back home. He had found a good job in the city, making good money while learning a trade. Dad liked where things were going; I guess mom did not.

By the time I was 18 months, they were divorced.

God's Planned Outcome

Despite the circumstances, God created me on purpose for a purpose. He could have denied my parents but instead He chose me to be a part of their lives. Although I did not go to church, little by little, my relationship with God grew, first through my grandparents, then through the Bible. As I grew a bit older, He revealed hidden secrets, such as the existence of my sister, which remained tucked away in my mind for decades to come. He also showed me why my mother built a wall so high that no one could get in. I didn't know it back then, but fast forward 20 years and that back story revealed God's wonderful plans of restoration. Keep reading. There is much left to share, but I promise it is going to be worth the ride!

God's Holy Word

For you formed my inward parts; you knitted me together in my mother's womb. (Jeremiah 139:13 ESV)

For I know the plans I have for you", declares the LORD, "plans to prosper you and not to harm you, plans to give you hope and a future. (Jeremiah 29:11 ESV)

Questions to Reflect On

1. Do you recall the first time you felt connected to God?
2. Looking back, can you pinpoint a time when God was trying to reach out, but you did not make the connection?
3. Do you have any family secrets that could explain things that occurred in your life?

UNBROKEN CHAINS

I n the previous chapter, I shared how my grandmother abandoned my mom and that it appeared my mother hated her for not being there during her childhood. I had a different experience. By the time I came along, my grandmother was present, and I thought she was amazing. She used to pick up my brother and me on the weekends to go to carnivals, movies, stores, parks, and restaurants. Anything just to hang out. My grandmother was an excellent seamstress. She made many of her own clothes. I remember her having reams of fabric stowed away in a large trunk. It was fascinating to see so much colorful fabric in one place. I had never been to a fabric store, so grandma's stockpile of fabric was impressive. She taught me everything from crocheting with my finger to sewing with the sewing machine. We bonded over many a pattern and she always saved fabric for me. I loved hanging out with her.

In my opinion, my mother wasn't overly sold on her mother's transformation, so she allowed only occasional visits, which made me treasure our time even more.

Grandma Charlotte had a relative who was a genealogy guru. Have you ever traced your lineage? Perhaps documented your ancestry or created a genealogy tree? This was back in the 1980s before genealogy websites and DNA kits, which would have made the process a whole lot easier.

Other than my grandmother and one uncle on my mother's side, I never met any of that side of the family. To learn that I had an entire group of people potentially like me was exciting, but also sad because I would probably never connect with any of them.

Through reading I found there are some impressive individuals in my family line. Every page seemed filled with service members, doctors, lawyers, and teachers. I chuckled to see so many members who made, lost and made fortunes again. In fact, my family was one of the richest families in the territory known as Milwaukee, Wisconsin today.

Most exciting was to see a relative who was quite good at playing the string bass. So good he went to Juilliard School of Music and played with the New York City Orchestra for many years. Why so exciting? I tried to play an instrument when I was younger, two of them in fact, the French horn and the clarinet. After a combined total of one month of trying, my music teacher suggested I find another activity because playing an instrument was not for me. This was the first time I felt failure.

Fast forward 35 years…guess what instrument my 15 year-old son plays, yes, the string bass! In a strange way I felt vindicated, now I could confidently tell my son that he gets his talent from my side of the family. Thank you, Jesus, for passing on those gifted genes.

You are probably wondering why all the genealogy talk. There is a point to my madness, I promise.

The revelation for me was watching the history and pattern of my family's dysfunction unfold. What caused my grandmother to have a child out of wedlock in the 1940s and to leave her kids in the 1950s? When did the chains get wrapped around us binding us up tighter and tighter? Did the enemy win out with his lies and deceit? God forbid.

As I see it, my grandmother suffered, my mother suffered, and I suffered. Grandma Charlotte had a daughter out of wedlock in 1949; my mother got pregnant with a daughter in 1969; and I got pregnant with a daughter in 1985 (more about that later).

The chains didn't stop with conceiving children before marriage; divorce ran in our family too. My grandmother was divorced. I appears my mother was married three times and divorced three times before she was 39. I was married three times and divorced twice before I was 26. An embarrassing fact I do not like to share.

We all started our youth and adult lives tied down by what seemed like one hurt after another. And those chains of pain stayed tied tight for decades. I didn't understand it back then and I don't really think I recognized the pattern of destruction until well into my 30s.

I used to think pain and hurt were just my lot in life, my destiny. I recall as a child never getting excited about anything. I was afraid that if I got excited then something bad would happen like the universe had this great plot against me. I never wanted to be disappointed, so I learned not to look forward to anything. It seemed easier that way.

You are probably wondering how God could have a plan for all this dysfunction? I can tell you that He did--and He still does.

God's Planned Outcome

In the case of my family, brokenness and dysfunction were not surprises to God. Free will allowed my family and myself to make poor choices that took us down a wrong path. The good news is that God can straighten out any crooked path to get us back on track right where we belong. Look at Biblical genealogy and those we see as heroes: Abraham, Isaac, and Jacob. Sure, you hear of all the great stories of accomplishment, but brokenness and dysfunction existed in those families too. We can't deny that God used those broken and dysfunctional families to accomplish His great purpose! Praise be to God that He knows the plan! He transformed those broken people and He can transform us too!

God's Holy Word

Since we did not really know God and certainly did not have a relationship with him while on the wrong path, we missed some key guidance from Him. Here is scripture to keep you going in the right direction.

Whoever heeds instruction is on the path to life, but he who rejects reproof leads others astray. (Proverbs 10:17 ESV)

Offer to God a sacrifice of thanksgiving, and perform your vows to the Most High, and call upon me in the day of trouble; I will deliver you, and you shall glorify me. (Psalms 50:14-15 ESV)

Consider it pure joy, my brothers and sisters, whenever you face trials of many kinds, because you know that the testing of your faith produces perseverance. Let perseverance finish its work so that you may be mature and complete, not lacking anything. If any of you lacks wisdom, you should ask God, who gives generously to all without finding fault, and it will be given to you. (James 1:2-5 NIV)

Questions to Reflect On

1. Did you grow up in a dysfunctional family? What type of dysfunction did you experience?
2. Were you surprised to learn that God uses all people, even broken and dysfunctional people for His glory?
3. How does knowing that God is in control give you peace about your situation? Does it give you hope that you can change things?

MOTHER'S OBSESSION

At the age of 23, I think, my mother married her third husband. This is the man I considered my dad since the time I was about three years old. Don't get me wrong, I never stopped loving my biological father, I just did not get to see him every day like I did my stepfather.

My mother married my stepfather to give us stability. She wanted a good life for me and she wanted to make a change for herself. Marrying him gave us stability but did not fix the issues I had with her. For some reason, we never truly connected. She confessed, usually when she was upset about something, that she never really wanted kids, but birth control didn't exist back then. I don't think she meant it.

At times, my mom wanted to be a good mother but didn't know how. Since she never had a real childhood, I think she was trying find herself, which resulted in times when she would become selfish and reclusive.

I was young, but I recall my mom taking on several different jobs. For a while, she worked at a nursing home with my stepfather's mom. There she served as a dietician, ensuring residents received meals appropriate for their health needs. My mom left the nursing home when she landed a great job at InSinkErator, which really helped the family. InSinkErator is known for creating garbage disposals. If you have a garbage disposal in your sink look at the ring on the drain, I bet it is stamped with the InSinkErator name.

Although working for a prominent company making pretty good pay was great for the family finances, Mom worked second shift, so it put a lot of responsibility on me. By the time I was nine years old, I cooked, cleaned, and watched my younger brother.

My mom worked late usually getting home at 11:00 p.m. which meant I only saw her on the weekends. The job did not help my relationship with my mom.

At some point in the late 1970s, my mom discovered body building. There were not a lot of women in the sport, except the females who (in my opinion) looked like men. So, my mom had to pave the way. I never saw her work so hard at anything before she made the leap into the sport. It was the first time in my life I remember being proud of my mom. I was proud of her for working so hard. It was also the first time in my life where I made the connection that if you work hard for something you can earn a reward for your effort.

Mom embraced every aspect of bodybuilding from proper nutrition and training to vitamins and supplements. She documented everything she ate, captured her training regimen, and even recorded her body changes. As she saw her body transform, she became more obsessed with the endeavor.

Bodybuilding took my mother away on the weekends too. She was dedicated and determined. She found her passion. She won several competitions, including first place for her height and weight group in my hometown. My mom once brought home a trophy that was almost as tall as my 7-year-old brother. She was well known in the circuit. She even had a personalized license plate: I Win 2.

My stepfather was also big into bodybuilding. He worked out and transformed his body into a well chiseled physique. Unlike my mother, he was what you would classify as a powerlifter. He was not a big guy, only standing about 5'8 but a solid 200 pounds with almost no body fat. When my dad walked into a room, you knew it. He was full of life with a personality that you could not miss, and a transformed body that intimidated many.

The weight training helped both of my parents. Mom found her niche and something she could call her own; Dad found new strength, which played out well in sports. He became a better softball player, running longer and hitting farther. Hitting the ball out of the park became the norm. He was untouchable.

While my mother worked, my father shuttled my brother and me all over the place. We were always on the go and, like my dad, my brother and I were both active in sports too.

There was never a dull moment, and thanks to dad we didn't stay home much. We were a go, go, go kind of family. The three Musketeers.

To this day, I still eat and walk quickly, habits formed all those years ago thanks to my dad.

My parents worked out in a gym owned by several members. It was basically a hole in the wall with mirrors and free weights everywhere--no machines. It was an old school set up where you pumped real iron. My mom was the only female and she loved it. They pushed her and she pushed them. I can recall a time when my mom tied a 25-pound weight around her waist and proceeded to crank out 15 pull ups in what seemed like seconds. I also remember the guys spotting her as she free-weight squatted 700 pounds for the first time. It was cool to see my mom, a little 5'2, 140-pound woman take care of business.

My mom's obsession for the sport grew, which took a toll not only on my relationship with her but also on my father's. Other than the gym, they were not spending much time together. Every waking moment for my mom was spent working out.

I remember asking my father why he loved my mother.

She wanted to be at the gym, not home with us or participating in anything we were doing. Without hesitation, he would always say he loved her because she was the love of his life.

As a teenage girl, I couldn't grasp that concept, especially since my mom and I were often at odds with one another.

God's Planned Outcome

Sometimes we become obsessed with things that make us feel good, seeking to fill a void that only God can fill. No matter how hard we try, unless we seek God, that emptiness will exist forever. To put God first is key. However, fixating on things of this world can be damaging and lead us away from God and toward our own selfish desires. In this situation, God was showing me the dangers of fixation, but was also teaching me about hard work, determination, and love. He helped me to see my mom in a different light. I learned that if you work hard at something you are rewarded. Mom's determination taught me to endure when things get tough and not to give up just because things are hard. God uses everything to get us where we need to be!

God's Holy Word

But each person is tempted when he is lured and enticed by his own desire. Then desire when it has conceived gives birth to sin, and sin when it is fully grown brings forth death. (James 1:14-15 ESV)

Finally, brothers, whatever is true, whatever is honorable, whatever is just, whatever is pure, whatever is lovely, what ever is commendable, if there is any excellence, if there is anything worthy of praise, think about these things. (Philippians 4:8 ESV)

And whatever you do, in word or deed, do everything in the name of the Lord Jesus, giving thanks to God the Father through him. (Colossians 3:17 ESV)

Questions to Reflect On

1. Have you ever encountered a time when things were happening that you didn't quite understand?
2. How did you deal with it? Did you run from it or did you embrace it?
3. Looking back, can you see how God used that time to prepare you for a future event?

BROTHER'S TRAGEDY

I never thought anything would deter my mother from her bodybuilding obsession. That changed the day my brother got hurt.

In 1982, I was watching my 7-year old brother. We lived in the country, but I gave my brother permission to ride his dirt bike to a community across the field about a mile away. My brother was such a social person. He loved hanging out with friends and had no fear, even at such a young age, to trek out on his own to be around people. Being five years younger than me, he was a real pain. He was always picking on me. He once put a metal airplane with a pointed tail wing on the stairs knowing I would come down from my upstairs bedroom and step right on it. He loved a good laugh at my expense. So, if my brother wanted to leave the house for a while, I usually let him go so I could have a break from his pranks.

On this day, my mother was leaving for work. It was about 2:00 p.m. when I got a call that my brother had been in a horrible accident.

My brother was run over by a kid on a riding lawn mower. Thank God my mom was still home when the call came in because at 12-years-old, I don't think I could have handled the situation too well on my own.

When mom and I arrived at the scene, my brother was laying on the ground covered in blood. He lost a big toe on one foot and the other foot was held together by a vein – his toes were detached in his shoe. My brother was wearing those popular brown suede shoes with the big gum soles which, to this day, I believe saved his feet from being completely cut off.

The ambulance had just arrived, and the paramedics were about to load my brother into it. My mom was screaming hysterically. I think she was yelling at the mother of the kid who ran my brother over. I stared in disbelief at my brother, who was in shock looking at his watch and apologizing for being late coming home. He found a broken watch at my grandmother's house the day prior and had been wearing it when he was hurt. Not really knowing how to tell time, he wore it anyway, and in his state of shock and hearing my mother screaming, thought he was late and in trouble.

I felt sick and numb. I can't stand the sight of blood and it seemed to be everywhere. My brother was wearing a yellow shirt and brown pants and they were both covered in little red dots of blood. If I had not known what happened, I would have thought someone shot him with a paint ball gun.

I remember being told to get into the ambulance and hearing the sirens going off. The journey to the hospital was going to be a difficult one. The paramedics were fast at work. One guy ripped off my brother's pants, wrapped his feet, and hoisted his leg up, while the other paramedic started IVs and pain meds. My brother was still apologizing to my mother. I then heard the drivers say they had a problem. There were two ways to get to the hospital from the location of the accident. One road was a short, direct trek, while the other was about five miles long. The longer route went around the city and would take 20 minutes to get to the hospital. My brother was losing so much blood that we needed to take the direct path. The problem was that the road had just been torn up to make way for a new, expanded highway. The demolished road appeared impossible to pass, but the paramedics decided we had to risk it if my brother was going survive.

The road was so bumpy. We were told to brace ourselves so that we would not fall on my brother, but as the ambulance made its way up the road, my brother was flopping around so much that the paramedics told us to help hold him still. We literally laid on my brother to keep him stable, a hard task to do without touching his injured feet.

After what felt like hours, we finally made it to clear road and then to the hospital where the staff was waiting outside to take my brother into surgery. My father was standing at the entrance of the hospital waiting as we pulled up. He saw my brother and completely lost it. I think that was the first time I saw my father cry and beg God for help.

My parents and I were whisked into the waiting area where many aunts, uncles, and cousins were waiting. I don't recall how long the surgery lasted, but I remember being told that one of the top vascular surgeons just happened to be in the area and was working on my brother. That appeared to give my parents some hope.

I don't know if I was still in shock, but all I could think about was guilt I felt for not wanting my brother around. I blamed myself for letting him go out and play. I blamed myself for calling my brother a pain, and I blamed myself for not being a better sister. I prayed to God to let my brother live and I would be better.

Praise be to God my brother survived the accident but had a long road to recovery. We were told that he might not walk again because he lost the ball joint of his foot. Of course, my mother laughed at the doctors. She told them he would be just fine, and she meant it. This is where all her obsession with bodybuilding paid off. At first, my parents took my brother to physical therapy but after a time, my mother decided she could do a better job with him at home--and she did. Not only did my brother walk again, but he also did so in record time. The accident happened at the end of the school year, and when it was time to go back to school, my brother was walking with crutches.

At first, the tragedy drew my parents closer, but after time, it caused their marriage to suffer. Blame games, fights over money, and drugs entered the picture. My mom's obsession become my brother, while my dad couldn't handle seeing his only son suffer. I don't think he ever overcame the initial shock and trauma of it all.

As my brother was healing, a lawsuit was moving forward to hold the guilty party accountable. My parents did not share anything about the lawsuit, but I overheard their conversations. My parents won a significant settlement for my brother and invested the money so that he would have something to live on when he was older.

The stress of everything took a toll on my dad. He began drinking more and smoking marijuana. My dad was changing before my eyes and it was scary. Up to that point, he could do no wrong.

My mother would devour any resource that she could find on healing and health to give my brother the advantage and a future.

After nearly losing his son, my father wanted my brother to enjoy life. Dad kept telling Mom to pull out some of the settlement money but she wouldn't, insisting that it was for my brother. Dad kept telling her it would be used for him.

Dad wanted to take family vacations and buy things, but Mom wouldn't budge. She knew the money would be needed for my brother's follow-up surgeries, if needed, and potential future issues.

Throughout this ordeal, my role had changed. I now tolerated everything my brother did; in my eyes, he could do no wrong. I went from considering him a pain to becoming his second mother, following him around, giving into his every whim, and standing watch over him. Nothing would ever hurt my brother again while I was around. My brother enjoyed the attention and was spoiled by us all.

God's Planned Outcome

Little did I know that God was using this tragedy for another life event my brother and I would experience five years later. You will read about that life altering event in Chapter 6. What happened to my brother was not a surprise to God. He was not punishing an innocent 7-year-old. This is an example of a time when things just happen. However, nothing in life is ever wasted. God uses every lesson to teach us and prepare us for things to come. This event sure did prepare me. I grew closer to my brother through this tragedy. I don't think I ever loved anyone as deeply as I loved him at that moment in time. This was also the first time I learned to give selflessly to someone in need. The day my brother was hurt was no different than any day before, but I learned to appreciate life because you never know when your number will be called.

God's Holy Word

Yet you do not know what tomorrow will bring. What is your life? For you are a mist that appears for a little time and then vanishes. (James 4:4 ESV)

So teach us to number our days that we may get a heart of wisdom. (Psalm 90:12 ESV)

Let all that you do be done in love. (1 Corinthians 16:14 ESV)

Who comforts us in all our affliction, so that we may be able to comfort those who are in any affliction, with the comfort with which we ourselves are comforted by God. (2 Corinthians 1:4 ESV)

Questions to Reflect On

1. Was there a time in life when you can recall a significant change to the way you viewed life?
2. How did your perspective on life change?
3. Did this newfound perspective help transform you into the person you are today?

ANOTHER LINK IN THE CHAIN

F ast forward to 1984. My brother continues to receive all the attention and, although I try to not feel disconnected, I am. Teenage hormones are racing; one day I am extremely happy, and the next day I am feeling alone and sorry for myself.

My parents seemed to be in a better spot now that my brother was excelling, so I did not want to rock the boat by sharing my feelings. Instead, I gravitated to a high school wrestler at school. He was handsome and caught the attention of all the girls.

I, on the other hand, did not see myself as attractive. The year prior, I got both glasses and braces. I felt anything but cute, but that boy seemed to gravitate toward me too. He would follow me around school. One of my cousins was dating his cousin so eventually we met and hit it off right away. It was a story of dysfunction meeting dysfunction. Turns out he grew up in a broken home too. His parents were divorced and he was living with his mother and her alcoholic, drug-addicted boyfriend. His mother was beautiful and could have had any guy she wanted; I never understood why she was with him, my guess is she was depressed and also an alcoholic. Being left with four kids to raise on her own took a toll on her life. To add fuel to the fire, her daughter got pregnant and she was left to raise that grandson. She once confessed that she just didn't want to be alone. I guess she settled. I thought his mother was a beautiful soul who just got the raw end of the deal when it came to life.

At 15 years old I was not allowed to date. In fact, when I asked my parents if I could date the new boy I met, they freaked out and forbade it, which led to three months of sneaking around. I was a latchkey kid, so the boy would ride the bus home with me, sneak into my house, hide in the attic until my father left to work out, and then hang out with me and my brother. My brother always threatened to tell on me.

He didn't have to, though, because I ended up pregnant. I was terrified of my parents and hid my pregnancy for seven months. Mom found out when she took me to my pediatrician. I had thrown up at breakfast and she thought I had a stomach bug. The pediatrician told my mom he thought I might have a tumor. I think he knew about the pregnancy but didn't want to tell her. Instead he sent us to the second floor to be seen by a gynecologist who informed my mother that I was pregnant.

My mom yelled a few choice words in front of the doctor and many more on the ride home.

Without going into too much detail, my parents decided it was best that I marry the father of my child. My mom confronted his mom and made it clear that her son would either marry me or never see his child because I would be sent to live with my biological father in Michigan. His mom agreed to the marriage.

On June 19, 1985, my mom escorted me into the court-house, signed the document giving me away, and left the building. I remember standing there, wondering what would happen next. I literally just got married and had nowhere to go. My new mother-in-law suggested that I live with her. I lived with my husband in her home for about 6 weeks.

What a turn of events. I was 16, pregnant and married. My husband and I were the only married couple in high school. And the school system had no idea what to do with us. We didn't know what to do with us.

On June 26, 1985, I gave birth to a beautiful baby girl. My daughter was two months early, weighing in at 3 pounds, 9 ounces, and was 16 inches long. She had to stay in the hospital for six weeks. My heart broke. About a week after giving birth to her, my father had my aunts and mother pack up my things and move me out of my mother-in-law's house. He couldn't stand the fact that I was not living with family and decided it was better for us to stay with his mom, my grandmother. I was relieved.

I had no car and walking to the hospital to see my daughter was hard because we had to walk quite a distance and because we had to walk through the bad side of town. Dad made me a butterfly knife on a machine at work and said to carry it with me just in case. I grew up going to my grandmother's house and hanging out in the street so honestly, I wasn't afraid. Well, maybe a little, but I was more determined to see my child than afraid of what could happen.

Finally, the day came when I could bring my daughter home. My aunt babysat my daughter while my husband and I went to school. The first time my dad saw my girl his heart melted. From that point on there was nothing he wouldn't do for her.

Eventually, my husband and I had saved up enough to get our own apartment for $245 a month. It was a good feeling to have our own home. It was a studio apartment and we slept in the living room, but it was ours. We still had no car and walking to school was freezing in the Wisconsin winters. My aunt was too far away to continue babysitting, so my mother-in-law took over. We would bundle up our daughter in the stroller, put a large comforter over the buggy, walk five city blocks to drop her off at my mother-in-law's house, and then walk another mile to get to school.

When my dad found out about our daily ritual, he was upset. How dare we take his grand-baby out like that in the cold. From that point on, he drove across town to pick us up to ensure his baby didn't get cold and then took us to school.

Eventually, he allowed my husband to drive him to work and to take the car (though my husband didn't have a license).

In June 1987, to everyone's surprise, we graduated high school. With no job prospects lined up and no money to go to college, my dad decided that it was time to have a heart-to-heart talk with my husband. Well, truth be told, he picked my husband up one day, drove him across town to the Navy recruiting location, and told him to not come out of the building until he was signed up for the Navy. My husband was terrified of my father so he did as he was told and joined the Navy.

While my husband spent the summer in bootcamp, my daughter and I stayed in Michigan with my biological father and grandmother.

God's Planned Outcome

God's will for us is very different from our own freewill. Humans are selfish by nature. God has a destiny for all of us but our freewill tends to get in the way. Don't be fooled; God always has a purpose and can redirect our bad decisions to get our lives back on track. It doesn't matter how much we deviate from His greater plan for our lives. At the time, I didn't know how my life would unfold, but God did. God is never surprised and has no uncertainty about what is to come. He knows the future. He blessed me with a daughter, which meant having the husband that would play a role in that process. I moved to Virginia, and he brought people into my life who would become instrumental to my future, including a woman who led me to Him.

God's Holy Word

I am the LORD; that is my name; my glory I give to no other, nor my praise to carved idols. Behold, the former things have come to pass, and new things I now declare; before they spring forth I tell you of them. (Isaiah 42:8-9 ESV)

But I the LORD will speak what I will, and it shall be fulfilled without delay. For in your days, you rebellious people, I will fulfill whatever I say, declares the Sovereign LORD. (Ezekiel 12:25 NIV)

Questions to Reflect On

1. Have you made decisions that did not align to God's will for your life?
2. How has God redirected you to align you back to His plan for your life?
3. Can you see the transformation God has made in your life?

DECEIT, DESTRUCTION, DEATH

ometime between June and September 1987 my
parents got divorced. I knew things had gotten bad
between them, but when I left for Michigan, they
were married, and when I returned, they were not. It was
depressing and strange at the same time; although they were
divorced, my dad still had a key to the house and came by
every day. He used the excuse that he had to bring my brother
home from school, which I imagine, in his mind, gave him the
right to come in the house.

My stepfather had an affair; however, he could not accept
the divorce. He was now living with his mom and every time I
would visit him; he would tell me he would never marry
another woman. He planned to marry Mom again. I remember
telling him that he might want to tell her that because she had
other plans.

My mom was in a different place. She was trying to move to California to live with a friend she met. I think she just wanted to get as far away from Wisconsin as possible. After 17 years of marriage, she wanted a fresh start. She tried to put the house up for sale, but every time she would put the real estate sign in the yard, my dad would knock it down or throw it away. He told her she could not take his son away.

She offered to give him sole custody of my brother, but that did not appease him. He didn't want Mom to go; he had plans to restore their marriage, but she wasn't having any of it. She even started dating someone else to prove her point, she was moving on.

Dad was furious with her dating, especially since he knew the guy she started seeing. He threatened the guy, who promptly dropped my mom.

I was on my dad's side; I wanted my family back together. Even though I had not lived at home in two years, and despite their dysfunction, we were still a family. Deep down, I thought if my mom could just forgive him, things would get back to normal--our normal anyway--and it would be okay.

Normal was no longer an option. In September 1987, my husband was home on leave from bootcamp. We stayed at my childhood home with my mom while we were planning our move to Virginia.

On September 23rd, my husband and I had a yard sale to raise money for our trip to Virginia. Around 4 p.m. we packed up our things and I tallied up the earnings. I miscounted and thought my brother had taken $20 from me. I jumped to this conclusion because the day prior, he got in trouble for taking $20 from my mom's purse for school lunch. In my mind, it was a natural assumption. Heartbroken that I would blame him for stealing, he took off on his bike for our cousin's house.

We were watching TV that evening when my dad stopped by as usual. I loved my dad and was happy to see him. My daughter ran to him as soon as he walked in the door. She loved her grandpa and he adored her. I couldn't understand why my mom couldn't forgive him and just remarry him already. Having been gone for most of the summer, I had not seen how bad things had gotten. I grew up with abusive language but had not realized how things escalated. My parent's fighting had gotten worse. I found out from my brother that my dad didn't like my mom dating and had attacked her one day in a drunken moment. My brother jumped on his back to stop him and my mother called the police.

On this day, as we watched TV my dad went to the bathroom. My mom ran over to me and asked me to hide his keys. I didn't want to get involved in this stuff; I was tired from the yard sale and feeling bad for accusing my brother of stealing.

After my dad finished using the bathroom he walked straight into the bedroom. I assumed they were making up. They did that often. They fought hard and loved hard too. Not on that day. On that day, he was not welcome in her room. On that day, he forced his way in. I do not know what happened behind closed doors, but as soon as the door swung open, my dad walked out looking disheveled, fixing his hair and buttoning up his shirt. My mom ran out in a robe hitting him. He walked outside, and she ran back in the room and got dressed, then came out of the bedroom with my dad's medallion in her hand, flashing it in front of the picture window. I later found out that the medallion, with Mary holding baby Jesus on it, was a gift to Dad from my grandmother. The medallion used to fall off the chain all the time because my dad never bought a new clasp.

Dad stopped his car and came back into the house. As he entered the house she ran back into the bedroom and locked the door. He beat on the door several times. I thought for sure he was going to break it down. He then ripped the chain off his neck and threw it at the door and told her to give it to her boyfriend to. He hit the door one more time and walked away.

My mom came out of the bedroom when the yelling stopped. I don't know what she thought but I don't think she expected him to be standing there. When my dad heard the door open, he turned slightly to look back, and there, holding a 9mm handgun, was my mother. Before I could assess the situation, my mother shot my dad right in front of us: my husband, my two-year-old daughter, and me. I think I went into shock because the whole situation became surreal. My mind could not process what just happened.

Shaking, my mother accidentally shot again, this time in the air. Somehow my fight or flight reaction kicked in because

I jumped up and stood in front of her, thinking she might shoot again. I was terrified. I thought she would kill us all.

I asked her what she did to my dad (not in those nice words) and she coldly said, "he pushed me too far." I could not process what she meant.

My mom left the scene before the police arrived. I waited with my father, praying he would live. He was turning purple but still had a pulse. I didn't realize he had a large hole in the back of his head, and being in shock, I couldn't see the vast amounts of blood pouring out and pooling up the floor.

After praying for my father, I ran to the phone. I dialed 911 only to realize the city where I lived didn't have 911 you had to dial the police department's number. I grew frustrated and threw down the phone. I was in hysterics. We must get my dad help. My husband, daughter and I ran out of the house to a stranger's house. The elderly women would not help us. I am sure I had blood on me and was not making sense. Looking back, I probably would not have opened the door to hysterical teenagers either. In any event, she must have called the police because they arrived at my house. Relieved, my husband and I quickly approached the police at the house door asking if they caught my mother. The police were oblivious. They had no clue what I was talking about and looked at us suspiciously.

As the paramedics carried my dad out of the house, my brother arrived home. He was screaming to see our dad. I couldn't let him in the house to see our father that way; it took both my husband and me to hold him back.

My father was rushed to the hospital, and we were rushed to the police station for interrogation, finger printing, and gun residue checking. Although I kept telling the police my mother shot my father, the police didn't know, so we were all tested. While at the police station, we got word that my father died.

My stepfather was Hispanic and from a big family; he was one of 12 kids. For 17 years he was my dad, but on that day, several of his brothers disowned me and I became my mother's daughter instead of my father's girl. One brother threatened to kill me before the night was over. Despite the passing time, I think I was still in shock, so the threats didn't even matter. I didn't care if I lived or died that day. I was lost.

In one day, I went from having a very large family to having only my husband and daughter.

The papers from Chicago to Milwaukee printed the story. It was a high-profile case because my mom was a competitive body builder. I could not escape the tragedy. I stopped watching TV and reading the paper so that I could pretend this horrible event never happened. The media drama went on for what seemed like months. The news was quick to report on every little detail. New evidence, the funeral, the family, everything. I couldn't escape it.

In October, my husband and I moved to Norfolk, Virginia, but flew back to Wisconsin to prepare for trial against my mother. We were both witnesses and had to testify against her.

I hated my mom at this point. I couldn't wrap my brain around what happened; I blamed her for everything. I felt that she was the cause of my pain not my dad despite his role in the ordeal and I thought she was to blame for destroying my life. It was her fault I had no one. I was empty, depressed, and broken.

God's Planned Outcome

As you can imagine, this was a hard story to share and even harder to reflect on. It took me back to a time I wanted to forget, but not sharing would mean I didn't acknowledge God's presence as I experienced it during the tragedy. It is important to state that God doesn't cause tragedy. God is love. But as we all know bad things happen in life. In fact, Jesus warns us that we will have trials in this life, but He is with us and has overcome them. God was with me that day. Not only did He send my brother away so he would not witness the tragedy, but I believe he also was sent away for his safety; protection for him. I adored my brother and to hurt him with my words was not something I ever sought to do. The only explanation was that my brother needed to be far away from home at that moment in time. I am also confident that God protected my eyes from the scene. I nearly faint at the sight of blood. Truly I tell you I never saw one drop of my father's blood. I learned after the fact that blood was everywhere. The walls were splattered with it and the carpet where my father laid (that was removed for evidence) was blood-soaked. In that moment, God spared me. He was with me. He gave me to the courage to lay on the ground holding my father's hand. Although I had not yet formed a relationship with God, I knew enough to cry out to Him in prayer. I knew that He existed and knew that He was the only one who could fix what happened. I begged God to let my father live and, in that moment, I felt my father's pulse. It was not strong, but it was there, showing me that despite not speaking, Dad was still present. I have no clue what my father thought as he laid there, but I know beyond a shadow of a doubt that my father heard me cry out to God. He heard me fight for his life. He heard me tell him I loved him and felt that love. I take comfort in knowing God didn't let him suffer, but instead He welcomed Dad home that day.

God's Holy Word

I have said these things to you, that in me you may have peace. In the world you will have tribulation. But take heart; I have overcome the world. (John 16:33 ESV)

He refreshes my soul. He guides me along the right paths for his name's sake. Even though I walk through the darkest valley, I will fear no evil, for you are with me; your rod and your staff, they comfort me. (Psalm 23:3-4 NIV)

For God so loved the world, that he gave his only Son, that

whoever believes in him should not perish but have eternal life. (John 3:16 ESV)

Questions to Reflect On

1. Have you dealt with a situation that is difficult to share with others?
2. What keeps you from sharing with others? Are you afraid of what others might think if you shared your ordeal with them?
3. Does reading this story give you any peace in knowing that even in the toughest times God is with us?

DRAMA IN THE COURTROOM

The day came when my husband and I were to testify in court to a judge, jury, and room full of other people. Thinking about it even now—more than 30 years later–it still gives me chills.

The trial was chaotic with lots of drama. Both of my grandmothers, my dad's mom and my mom's mom were present and in the front row. On the first day of the trial before the proceedings, my mom's mom offered condolences to my dad's family. She was heartbroken too. She loved my dad; he was the reason my mother and her were on speaking terms and the reason she survived cancer.

Many years earlier my grandmother sought a relationship with my mother, who was harboring feelings of resentment and abandonment and wouldn't hear of it. My dad convinced her to give her mother a chance. He came from a large

Hispanic family that was very close and he adored his mother. Somehow my mom relented and made amends. At this point, she had not forgiven my grandmother but was at least willing to try to get to know her.

For as long as I can remember, my grandmother was in my life. She would pick my brother and I up on the weekends just to spend time with us. I suppose it was a way to show my mother she had changed. I am not quite sure. What I do know is I loved spending time with my grandmother. She was fun to hang out with and I always felt her love.

Sometime in my early teens my grandmother got cancer. It was a pretty aggressive form with not much hope for recovery. My dad's father died of cancer a few years prior so he was able to offer plenty of advice and recommendations. He became an advocate and champion for my grandmother. My grandmother went through treatments, lost her hair, and became thinner, but the cancer didn't beat her. She survived, and she always thanked my dad for his help.

Watching my grandmothers interact in the courtroom was a bit strange. I didn't even know they knew each other. Before that day I had never seen them in the same room together. The conversation seemed to go well; both women cried, hugged, and took their seats.

The trial began.

The judge, jury, prosecutor, and defense attorney were all present. Even my mom was present, sitting at the table. There was a lot of discussion on who would testify first. I remember the defense attorney requesting that my brother speak, but my mom would not allow it. She was adamant that her 12-year-old son did not need to be further traumatized.

After what seemed like hours, I was called to the stand. I was the first person to testify.

I was prepared for the questions I knew were coming from the prosecutor, but not for the defense attorney's strange line of questioning. After several minutes of questioning about the actual incident, the attorney put up a large picture, almost life-size, of my father. It was one of my favorite pictures of my dad. He was wearing a blue track suit and had just come from a powerlifting competition, I think. A friend of his must have taken the picture a few years back.

The attorney then began to ask me questions such as:

"Can you define for the audience what a bodybuilder is? How about defining what a powerlifter is? What is the difference between the two?"

I could not understand why he was asking me non-case-related questions. What the heck is the point I kept thinking?

I discovered very quickly that he was trying to demonstrate how much bigger and stronger my dad was than my mom, to show that the incident was a result of years of domestic abuse.

The realization hit when the attorney started asking me questions about my life growing up. I don't recall the exact questions, but they were basically asking me if I ever saw my father strike my mother, yell at her, or hurt her. The questions seemed never ending.

I just wanted to tell my story of that day so that I could get off the stand. I was terrified of being up there and the prosecutor and attorney were forcing me to live the worst day of my life over and over again. I wanted to make it stop, get off that nightmare merry-go-round.

My stepfamily was crying, at times yelling and even booing. It was hard to look at my mom at the table. I was still reeling from what had happened and I thought my mom had snapped that day. Intense fear ran through me.

If my mom could kill a man whom she loved for nearly 17 years, would there be a time when she stopped loving me, and would she kill me as well?

Before I was released from the spotlight, the defense attorney threw up another picture. This one made me physically sick. I thought I was going to pass out. The picture was of my dad in the hospital with a large blue bag over his head. It must have been when the doctors were trying to save him. The picture was graphic, triggering flashbacks of me laying on the floor holding my dad's hand, feeling for a pulse. He kept turning darker and darker purple as I talked to him. The picture was another indicator to me that my dad did indeed die. Something I still was not handling very well.

The courtroom grew cold. I felt no warmth anywhere. There was so much anger and sadness in the room. No joy of any kind could be felt.

Everyone wanted a story. The media was there to get their scoop. Family wanted to hear every detail of what happened; most were in shock like I was. Strangers were present just to be part of the circus, I suppose.

My testimony was done. I was free to go but could not stay in the courtroom. As a witness, I was not allowed to hear the testimony of anyone else. I found that decision hard as I wanted to be there to make sure things were told correctly.

In the end, my mom got second degree murder and a sentence of 25 years in prison. Since she was a strong body-builder, the jury didn't accept the defense of domestic abuse. It was hard hearing my mother would be sent away for so long. One part of me was happy because of what she did, but as her daughter, the other part was sad because it meant the end of my family forever. I was grieving the loss of both of my parents now.

No one in my life at that moment understood what I was feeling. Only my brother could understand what it felt like to lose both parents, but even my brother didn't know how it hurt to be rejected. My dad was his biological father so he was welcomed by everyone. When my stepfamily looked at me, they no longer saw me, they saw my mom. They didn't mean to hurt me, but they were dealing with their own grief.

After the trial and back in Virginia, I learned I was pregnant with my second child. My daughter was born and didn't smile for nearly a year. The doctor said it could have been because I was depressed and experiencing a host of emotions while being pregnant during the trial. My three-year-old daughter was also traumatized. Remember she witnessed the death of my dad too. She kept walking around the house saying, "grandpa night night, boom." The psychologist said she would forget, and after about a year, she did.

God's Planned Outcome

It is often said that moms and daughters experience turmoil during the teenage years, but I think what we went through far surpassed any normal conflict. Testifying against my mother was one of the lowest points in my entire life; it was not normal at all. Doing the right thing meant further destroying my family. My testimony gave evidence to the jury, who gave a guilty verdict that would send my mom to prison for years. How did God have a plan for this situation? As I said before, nothing surprises God. He didn't put me in that situation, but he taught me about the importance of truth that day. As Christians, we must tell the truth even when it is hard. I didn't realize it at the time, but this was another test that would help me become the person I am today. I can also look back and see now that God can restore anything--for nothing is beyond His reach.

God's Holy Word

Blessed is the man who remains steadfast under trial, for when he has stood the test, he will receive the crown of life, which God has promised to those who love him. (James 1:12 ESV)

Beloved, do not be surprised at the fiery trial when it comes upon you to test you, as though something strange were happening to you. But rejoice insofar as you share Christ's sufferings, that you may also rejoice and be glad when his glory is revealed. (1 Peter 4:12-13 ESV)

When the righteous cry for help, the Lord hears and delivers them out of all their troubles. The Lord is near to the broken-hearted and saves the crushed in spirit. (Psalm 34:17-18 ESV)

Questions to Reflect On

1. Have you encountered a time when doing the right thing was hard but necessary?
2. Can you see how doing what was right helped form the person you have become today?
3. Has my testimony helped you realize that even during the most dire of times, God is still at work?

FORGIVENESS

Fast forward two years and my first marriage is falling apart. I think experiencing a traumatic event either pulls people together or rips them apart. For us, it completely ripped us apart. My husband became obsessive to the point that I had no freedoms, no friends, and no social life. I would equate his actions to a person with abandonment issues. At first, I tolerated it. I figured it was my consequence for marrying at 16. As time went by, I knew we would never be the same after that experience. I didn't feel safe with him.

We were both too young to realize that we needed counseling, and after fighting for so long, I finally threw in the towel. I didn't want to be married to him anymore. Perhaps he was another strong reminder of what happened that day; I don't know for sure. What I do know is our relationship no longer worked, and I needed to move on. I ran.

I quickly found husband number two. He was in the Navy and reminded me of a Puerto Rican Jean Claude Van Damme. He was a kick boxer and in great physical shape. He made me feel safe, which is what I needed at that time. To make a very long story short, the Navy moved us to Puerto Rico, his home country. At first, it was great living on a tropical island. The weather was amazing. A huge difference from growing up in Wisconsin. I thought I hit the jackpot. My husband loved me and my girls, and things were going well. I was so far away and could pretend the tragedy never happened. I was in another world and this scenario played well into my newfound pattern of running instead of facing problems.

My husband asked me about my mom and I shared. He asked why I would not forgive her and when I explained, he said, "Your mother is your mother no matter what": a statement that rang hard in my head. My dad used to say that to me every time my mom and I argued. He would say, "Your mother is your mother no matter what, you can have many fathers, but only one mother."

That statement now came to me every night as I slept. I would wake up in a cold sweat thinking my father was talking to me. It finally stopped the day that I told myself to reach out to my mother. I just needed the courage to do so. I didn't even know where to start; I didn't know what prison my mom was in and I had no idea how to contact her.

I started calling around and eventually found out the name of the prison where my mom was held. I called the prison and was told I needed to be on the list to reach my mom. If I wasn't on her list, I couldn't talk to her. How weird is that? A daughter can't talk to her mother because of some list. I explained the situation and the person on the phone passed a message to my mom. I was told to call back at a certain time and they would try to connect me with her.

I called back and my mom answered. I stated my name and was stunned by her reply: "Jeannine who?" "Uh, your daughter, Jeannine." The conversation was awkward at first but softened after a bit. I have no idea how long the first conversation was, but I remember crying a lot.

Over the next couple of years, we continued to talk by phone. She would tell me about things she was doing in prison, working at a job managing people in various work areas and going to college to earn an associate degree. She even helped a U.S. Senator with a domestic abuse bill.

After seven years of prison time my mother was released on good behavior.

She moved to Chicago, Illinois, and worked for an anti-aging organization run by one of the doctor's that served as her sports medicine doctor when she was bodybuilding.

Somewhere along the line, I left my second husband and moved back to Virginia. Turns out he loved me, and every other woman too. I decided it was time to make a change.

Back in the states and living with a friend I met when

working at a cable company, my life was a bit of a mess again. I was depressed from divorce number two and upset that I had to start all over again. I had left a great job before moving to Puerto Rico, and now I had to find something new. Having two little girls to care for made it imperative that I find work quickly. I signed up with a temp agency and was placed at a Christian law firm.

While working at the law firm I heard a lot about Jesus from coworkers. This was the first time in my life where people openly talked about God and the gospel. My curiosity grew so much that I ended tagging along to church with another friend I had known from a previous job. I went to church with her almost every Sunday and couldn't get enough Jesus. I was baptized at that church and sought out a new life for myself.

During this period in my life, I continued having conversations with my mother. Little by little, my heart softened, and I began to enjoy the thought of spending time with my mom. I visited her in Chicago, where I discovered she was struggling to feed herself. It was time to move her to Virginia with me; I was raising my two daughters on my own so we could both use the help. I made the trip to Chicago, got a trailer, and hauled her and her stuff with me to the beach.

Forgiveness did not happen overnight. I had lots of questions but was afraid to ask her anything because I didn't want to traumatize her. I was still pretending the tragedy never happened. I was finally in a good place (or so I thought) and I didn't want to have nightmares, deal with depression, or have anxiety again.

There were lots of things I had to teach mom, including what ATM's were. I never thought about what happens to a person when they live in a small, confined space for an extended period of time, or how they cope being around people who are always out to hurt them. Prison changed her personality and attitude.

The confident mom I grew up with didn't take crap from anyone, but she was no longer the same. She was tough, but there was also a different side that I had never seen before--an anxious, more cautious side. She no longer took chances or chased big dreams; she just seemed to exist.

As our connection grew, mom opened up about her experiences. She would share prison stories that terrified me. I couldn't imagine how she managed. When my mom entered prison, she was in top physical form and used that to her advantage. She found the biggest girl in the prison, told her to sit in a chair, and lifted her completely off the ground. People were shocked to see her strength. Mom said she found many ways to demonstrate her strength, so no one would mess with her. And it worked.

In Virginia with me, mom was not interested in body-building anymore; she focused on powerlifting and strength training now. She said she never wanted to feel weak in her life again. My mom felt comfortable in the gym for her the gym was church. She walked in and commanded respect, I recall a time when a big guy was bench pressing weight and my mom asked to jump in. He agreed and proceeded to take weight off the bar. Mom stopped him and told him to add about 25 more pounds to each side so that she could warm up. The guy left and we never saw him at the gym again.

As time went on, I discovered that I was forgiving my mom. I had a hard time forgetting but I no longer hated her. I wanted to help her. I craved a relationship with my mom and I missed my family, as dysfunctional as it was.

One day I came to the realization that forgiving my mom didn't mean I had to be okay with or forget what happened. I never would; what happened changed my life forever. But I didn't have to hurt from holding onto all the anger anymore.

I was at peace with my decision since, in a strange way, I felt my dad gave me permission to forgive her. Even in my dreams I could hear him saying, "your mother's your mother no matter what, your mother's your mother no matter what." I remember thinking, okay, dad! I choose to listen as I had done so many times before. I relent; I forgive her. I forgave my mom in 1994.

God's Planned Outcome

Forgiveness is hard. In my case, I felt hurt, betrayed, abandoned and depressed. This was not lost on God. He watched his son be hurt, betrayed, abandoned, and even killed. Yet even in that instance, God had a plan to bring salvation to the world. Jesus' death on the cross paid for our sins. As sinners, we all fall short, way short. We do terrible things to each other--some of which are irreversible and have long-lasting effects. But God gave us Jesus. God's planned outcome was set at the beginning of creation and fulfilled the day Jesus died on a cross for you and me. Jesus died to save us all, not just a select few. The only requirement is to believe in him. God doesn't destroy families, the enemy does. The enemy crept in and created havoc in my family the same way that he did to Adam and Eve's family. But God conquered the enemy through Jesus and gave me the victory. God taught me to forgive so that I could be freed from the clutches of the enemy and rest in God's promise of peace.

God's Holy Word

If you forgive those who sin against you, your heavenly father will also forgive you. (Matthew 6:14 NLT)

Anyone who does not love does not know God, because God is love. (1 John 4:8 ESV)

The Lord is not slow to fulfill his promise as some count slowness, but is patient toward you, not wishing that any should perish, but that all should reach repentance. (2 Peter 3:9 ESV)

Above all, keep loving one another earnestly, since love covers a multitude of sins. (1 Peter 4:8 ESV)

Questions to Reflect On

1. Is there anyone in your life that you have a hard time forgiving?
2. Does reading about my story help you move forward in forgiving the person that may have hurt you?
3. Do you understand that forgiving the person is for you not necessarily for them? Can you see that it frees you from the enemy who wants to keep you stuck and in pain?
4. Does wanting to defeat the enemy help you to forgive?

NEW BEGINNINGS

Being saved and rekindling a relationship with my mom did not instantly change me. I did not have a right relationship with God and at times, I felt like I was just going through the motions. I went to church and attended events, but that was it.

I even took my mom to church once. At the Christian law firm, I worked directly for the Chief Operating Officer who happened to be a local pastor. As a single mom with little ones, I was grateful that he would give me church work to do to earn extra money. For about a year, I created and printed the church bulletins for him.

One Sunday, I thought it would be a great idea to take my mom to church. After some persuasion, my mom agreed to go with me. I was so excited; maybe she would find God too.

Not quite. The pastor decided to talk about the Ten

Commandments, focusing specifically on Commandment #6: You shall not murder. I was horrified for my mom. There she sat, listening to the preacher condemn her. I know she felt singled out. She never went to church with me again and I couldn't blame her.

About three months after moving to Virginia, mom went to college. She had earned her associate degree in prison and was now working on her bachelor's degree. I was focused on doing a good job at work so that the company would hire me full-time, which they did.

I was also focused on getting my life back together. I started going out with friends, dancing and partying, but grew tired of the party life rather fast. Having been married at 16 and raising children gave me no real desire to continue the fast life. It was fun for a short moment but then it was done.

In 1996, some girlfriends and I were complaining at another friend's house that there were no good guys to be found. A visitor, a Navy Corpsman who happened to be in the room said, "You girls just don't know where to look. There are plenty of good guys out there." He then planned a cookout for the Fourth of July and told us girls to show up. We did, and the rest is history (at least for me).

At that cookout I met an incredible guy named Hayden who I dated for eight months before he was released from the Navy for medical issues. Hayden was diagnosed with IGA Nephropathy, a condition in which his kidneys would eventually fail requiring the need for a transplant. Hayden was sent back home to Georgia and we broke up. I was devastated but felt it was for the best. I had already been married twice, and I was not trying to jump into another marriage. I dated a couple of other guys for the next year and a half but nothing panned out. My heart just wasn't in it. Honestly, I still had feelings for Hayden.

One day Hayden's dad, Gary, called and invited me for a visit. I met Gary when he came to visit Hayden while we were dating. Gary and I hit it off. Gary was getting married on New Year's Eve and wanted me to be there.

I drove down to Georgia for the wedding, hoping that I would see Hayden. As it turned out, Hayden was living with his dad, so my wish was not a difficult one. Hayden greeted me at the door. I think Gary secretly wanted me there as a plan to see Hayden again. If that's true, then his plan worked because as soon as I saw Hayden my heart melted. Turns out Hayden's did too. By the end of my one-week stay we were dating again. Within three months, Hayden moved to Virginia and within a year we were married.

Life was moving along, which created one small issue. The house we lived in was becoming too small. I bought it as a single mom with two small girls, but now my mom was living with us, and the girls were outgrowing their bedroom and really needed to spread out. I told my mom it might be time for her to find a place of her own, which she did, except it was not in Virginia. She moved back to Wisconsin to be near her mother.

Things were going well for our family. Our daughters found friends in the neighborhood and started attending the church down the street.

I would like to say Hayden and I were attending church, but we weren't. We were just trudging along doing our own thing not thinking anything about God. Our daughters begged us to try the church, but most times Hayden would say no, and I went along with whatever he said. One day that changed. The girls asked again and, to my surprise, Hayden said yes and off to church we went.

We enjoyed church and found ourselves going more and more. I won't pretend we went every Sunday but we were there a lot more than we had been in the past, which was huge. I was rediscovering God and it felt good. At this time, I also transferred jobs from the Christian law firm to a full-time job at a Christian University, where I was surrounded by Christians and could attend worship in the middle of the day.

God's Planned Outcome

God continues to work in our lives, not just in the bad times but also in the good. He continued to grow our family and used our daughters to get us to go to church. We were like the lost sheep and as the Shepherd, He came to find us. He began to draw us closer and closer to Him.

God's Holy Word

He will tend his flock like a shepherd; he will gather the lambs in his arms; he will carry them in his bosom, and gently lead those that are with young. (Isaiah 4:11)

So he told them this parable: "What man of you, having a hundred sheep, if he has lost one of them, does not leave the ninety-nine in the open country, and go after the one that is lost, until he finds it? And when he has found it, he lays it on his shoulders, rejoicing. And when he comes home, he calls together his friends and his neighbors, saying to them, 'Rejoice with me, for I have found my sheep that was lost.' Just so, I tell you, there will be more joy in heaven over one sinner who repents than over ninety-nine righteous persons who need no repentance. (Luke 15:3-7 ESV)

Questions to Reflect On

1. Did God have to find you and bring you back into the fold?
2. How did you draw closer to God?
3. Where do you find hope for a new beginning?

HEARTACHE AGAIN?

Hayden and I got into our groove. By 2001, we both had good paying jobs, which afforded the opportunity to upgrade to a bigger house. While Hayden was out walking the dog, he found a perfect house right around the corner from our current home. It was a five-bedroom home on a corner lot with plenty of room for the kids. I had two daughters from my first marriage, but Hayden and I wanted at least one child together. We bought the house.

Soon after, in September 2001, I found out I was pregnant with a girl, Camryn. I was 32-years-old and nervous about my new situation. Remember, I was pregnant at 16 so that meant my oldest daughter was now 16-years-old. My youngest daughter was 13-years-old, so the age difference with the new baby was quite significant. The thought of starting over with diapers and drool also gave me anxiety. Had I made a terrible mistake? Did I roger up for something I really didn't want to do? What was I thinking?

At work, I was pregnant, my boss was pregnant, and my co-worker was adopting a newborn baby. It seemed like a great time to be pregnant. At least the support and camaraderie was there, right?

On September 10, 2001, I shared with my boss that I was nervous and confessed that I felt guilty about it. She calmed my fears and helped me see all the good that would come from the pregnancy.

The good thoughts were short-lived when our country was attacked the next day on 9/11. No longer was I concerned; instead I felt incredibly blessed to have the opportunity to have a child when other families were dealing with so much loss and uncertainty after the attacks.

I discovered quickly that having a child in your 30s is much different than in your 20s (or in my case, teens). My body did not seem to operate the way that it did in past pregnancies. Within three months, I had gained enough weight to warrant maternity clothes, which had not happened until the last month of my past pregnancies. I was just tiny by nature, but not anymore.

In November, my doctor informed me about various tests to check for things like down syndrome and other issues. About two weeks after the blood tests the results were in and the news was life-changing.

I remember Hayden was outside raking leaves and I was

making chocolate chip cookies. The house smelled wonderful and overall the day was awesome. I was no longer experiencing morning sickness, so life was good.

A phone call from the doctor changed my mood quickly. He told me the test results were in, and it looked like our daughter had Trisomy 18, something I thought must be a type of down syndrome. The doctor stated it was a fatal fetal anomaly meaning our daughter would not live. My thoughts raced. She looked great on ultrasound. Surely the tests were wrong; the doctor was wrong.

I went in for a 3D ultrasound, received an amniocentesis, and had genetic testing to confirm the results. The findings were confirmed: my daughter had Trisomy 18.

The news kept getting worse by the minute. As soon as the diagnosis was confirmed, the doctors who did the amniocentesis tried to convince me to abort my child. They shared scary facts about the condition to get me to terminate. True facts, such as Trisomy 18 babies do not move and can perish in the womb. The toxins can build up and endanger the mother's life.

Hayden and I had been married for only two and a half years. He vehemently said he wanted my life over the babies. I couldn't move past the thought of aborting my child. I thought God would punish me for such a decision. Hayden offered to take the punishment if it meant saving my life. I had to remind him that we are all judged individually on our actions.

I remember him reading his devotional the morning after the results were confirmed and telling me that God treasures all life--even Baby Camryn's. No matter what happened, she was created on purpose. At that moment, we prayed together and moved forward with our decision to keep our baby.

I was still working for the Christian University at the time. People prayed over me nearly every day. I felt loved. The ladies at work even threw me a baby shower, except they called it a blessing shower. They said no matter what Camryn was a blessing and deserved to be celebrated.

To the doctor's surprise, not only did I make it to the second trimester, but I also made it to the third. Something unheard of for a woman carrying a Trisomy 18 baby, who doesn't often make it to term. At 36 weeks pregnant, I gave birth to my daughter.

Camryn was born alive and had strong lungs. She cried loudly, letting the world know she arrived. She gave a good fight for 2 and a half days, then passed quietly while Hayden and I held her hands.

Losing a child is unbearable. I felt numb, weak and beside myself. I have very little recollection of planning the funeral, and even less of the actual service. I was present but not really there.

Going back to work after four weeks was tough. It got harder when a coworker told me that my daughter died because I didn't have enough faith. The fear of God that I had as a child grew even more now. My husband completely rejected God. He was angry. We stopped going to church.

Life continued. I thought our marriage was over because

Hayden and I couldn't even talk to each other. I was moving--albeit slowly--but he was going nowhere. I finally told him that if he didn't seek help, I was going to leave him. I couldn't take anymore sorrow in my life. I wanted to run away like I had done so many times before when forced to deal with the hard stuff.

Love won out, and Hayden sought help. He was put on an antidepressant, which worked wonders. Our relationship was back on track.

Six months later, another coworker told me that she had heard from God in a dream that I was going to have a son. Truthfully, I thought she lost her mind. I was still trying to hold it together from losing Camryn, and now someone was telling me I was going to go through this all over again? I don't think so.

Of course, God knows better than me, and on Cami's first birthday, I did indeed conceive a child – a son.

Hayden and I warmed to God again, thanked Him, and sought His hope for our lives. Back to church we went.

God's Planned Outcome

To lose a child is something I would not wish on my worst enemy. The heartache from the loss is overwhelming and at times unbearable. Not only did I lose my daughter, but I lost all the dreams and hopes I had for her, too. As a mother, the hardest part was never knowing she was okay. I longed to hold her, check on her, smell her, and watch her. My arms ached from the emptiness. Life felt unfair. Everywhere I turned, I found mothers with their babies. At the time I thought God was playing a cruel joke on me. I couldn't even go to church because mothers would bring their babies into the service. But God doesn't do anything to hurt us. He loves us; He does not want us to suffer. He knows what it feels like to lose a child. He watched His one and only innocent Son die on a cross for our sins. What God did in my situation was change my thinking. He spoke to my spirit and revealed that my daughter, Camryn, was okay, better than okay. He helped me see that she was sent for a purpose and her brief time fulfilled her mission. She existed to bring hurting people together in prayer. The unity and love felt by all through the situation still exists today. Seventeen years later, I still feel love from those who endured with me. God has also brought people into my life that I am able to help because of my experience. Everything God does is for a purpose.

God's Holy Word

Blessed be the God and Father of our Lord Jesus Christ, the Father of mercies and God of all comfort, who comforts us in all our affliction, so that we may be able to comfort those who are in any affliction, with the comfort with which we ourselves are comforted by God. For as we share abundantly in Christ's sufferings, so through Christ we share abundantly in comfort too. (2 Corinthians 1:3-5 ESV)

He heals the brokenhearted and binds up their wounds. (Psalm 147:3 ESV)

Many are the plans in the mind of a man, but it is the purpose of the Lord that will stand. (Proverbs 19:21 ESV)

Questions to Reflect On

1. Do you struggle with the loss of someone you love?
2. What do you struggle with the most?
3. Does knowing God has a purpose and a plan even in times of loss give you comfort?

LIFE AND DEATH

I would be lying if I said my pregnancy with Zachary was perfect. The first 20 weeks was very tense, not because of morning sickness, but because of uncertainty. At that point I did not know the gender of the child I was carrying, and the Trisomy 18 statistic stuck in my mind. More girls are affected by Trisomy 18 than boys, 3 to 1, in fact. I was so afraid I was going to have another girl and go through the loss all over again. I didn't have it in me to deal with more loss.

During this pregnancy, I passed a kidney stone, so my doctor sent me for an ultrasound of my kidneys and bladder. The ultrasound tech was so precious. She told me she could see the baby but was not allowed to tell me the gender. I busted out in tears, which completely caught her off guard. I explained my previous experience and begged to know. Poor girl didn't know what hit her. I was a blubbering cry baby. She left the room and returned with another young woman, and together they told me I was having a little boy. I hugged and thanked them profusely. They had no idea of the gift they had just given me. I went home and shared the good news with Hayden.

The following Monday, Hayden and I had to act surprised at the news of a boy during our scheduled ultrasound because we didn't want to get the ultrasound technicians at the previous place to get in trouble.

Overjoyed, I carried our son for the remainder of my pregnancy.

Life seemed perfect. Surely nothing else could happen, right? Wrong.

Hayden was medically discharged from the Navy when we were dating back in 1996. He had a condition called IGA Nephropathy, in which his kidneys would eventually fail, requiring the need for a transplant. In November 2003, my husband had a routine biopsy of his kidneys to see how they were functioning. The biopsy went well, and the doctor determined that Hayden had at least 80% of his kidney functionality remaining and that it would be at least 10 years before he would have to worry about his condition.

Thanksgiving came, and Hayden started feeling sick. He went to his primary care physician, who gave him antibiotics. Hayden continued to get worse. In December, my mom came to stay with me while Hayden and my youngest daughter traveled to Georgia for Christmas. I was eight months pregnant with Zachary and just couldn't handle the long road trip. I had gained about 50 pounds during the pregnancy and the extra weight was taking a toll on my back and hips.

When Hayden returned, he was even sicker. He went back to the doctor, who told him he had pneumonia and gave him more meds. The meds were not helping. At this point Hayden could not even lay down to sleep. He was forced to sit up in a chair to sleep or he would lose his breath.

I was getting concerned because he would not go back to the doctor. I called his mother in Nebraska for help. She showed up on our doorstep two days later. Three days later, my husband got violently ill. It turns out he didn't have pneumonia at all. His kidneys were failing and he was experiencing congestive heart failure. His kidney doctor said that he needed emergency dialysis immediately or he would die. Not exactly the way Hayden wanted to spend his birthday; he turned 30 years old on January 16, while being treated in the hospital.

One month later, our son was born. I was able to stay home with him while I was on maternity leave, but my time was divided between caring for Zach and taking Hayden to dialysis three times a week.

Hayden was approved to do home dialysis, which made things a little easier for us. Home dialysis meant that I was able to go back to work and Hayden could take care of our son. It seemed liked the perfect set...up until it was not.

Hayden ended up getting a rare and life-threatening infection, which promptly ended home dialysis. Zachary went to daycare, and Hayden was back to the dialysis clinic for treatment three times a week.

It wasn't working. Dialysis was not cleaning his blood enough, so he needed a kidney transplant sooner rather than later. I wanted to give him my kidney but was unable since I had just had our son. My mom stepped up and was set to give him a kidney, but a week before the surgery she backed out. She confessed later that she was afraid.

My husband was dying and there didn't seem to be any help in sight.

God's Planned Outcome

After going through so much tragedy in life, it almost seems foreign when things go right. The blessing of my son is a perfect example. I was not quite sure how to handle the blessing. It was also difficult to feel blessed when Hayden was walking through a time of trial. This situation taught me that despite our trials, God still provides blessings. We can experience both great joy and great sadness at the same time. Joy is not dependent on circumstances. God gives us joy freely no matter what is going on in our lives. I was able to be joyful with the blessing of my son and with the fact that my husband was still living.

God's Holy Word

Count it all joy, my brothers, when you meet trials of various kinds, for you know that the testing of your faith produces stead- fastness. And let steadfastness have its full effect, that you may be perfect and complete, lacking in nothing. (James 1:2-4 ESV)

Now faith is confidence in what we hope for and assurance about what we do not see. (Hebrews 11:1 NIV)

Rejoice always, pray continually, give thanks in all circum- stances; for this is God's will for you in Christ Jesus. (1 Thes- salonians 5:16-18 NIV)

Questions to Reflect On

1. Do you have a hard time experiencing joy when you are going through a trial?
2. What do you do when you experience a challenge? Do you run, pretend it doesn't exist, or turn to God?
3. Does knowing that joy is not circumstantial give you peace in knowing that when you encounter a trial in the future you will have the strength to endure?

HOPE RESTORED

I learned fast that when you try to control things, nothing seems to work out as planned. The realization hit me that there was absolutely nothing I could do I could not save my husband. His mom had gone through chemotherapy for breast cancer, so she was not allowed to donate. Other family members had a different blood type. Things were looking dire and my hands were tied.

I remember hearing my doctor, the one assigned to me for the transplant review, say he would not sign off on me to give Hayden a kidney, even if I was match. He found too much evidence to indicate that I would have lots of kidney stones in the future. It would not be wise to give up a kidney because I would need it one day. I was rejected as a donor.

I prayed harder than ever. I just could not believe God allowed my daughter to die and now was going to take my husband, too. I know that is not how God works, but back then I was emotionally exhausted. I didn't have much fight left in me.

One afternoon, I walked into work after lunch and broke down as soon as I hit the receptionist's desk. In my emotional state, I did not notice the new intern that I hired a few weeks earlier, crouched down filing paperwork. He popped up his head and asked if I was okay. Embarrassed and a bit annoyed, I explained my husband's situation. Perplexed, but with great confidence, he informed me he would give my husband a kidney.

Now I was really annoyed. I didn't have time for this nonsense. I even remember reminding him about the competitiveness of law school and how he needed to focus on his studies.

To my surprise, he stood up, and without skipping a beat, informed me he could do law school anytime, but this was someone's life we were talking about. He sure put me in my place.

The conversation ended with him telling me that he would get back with me the next day after he spoke to his mother and his fiancé back home. I acknowledged but didn't really believe anything would come of it. He was 21-years-old; how serious could he be?

Turns out he was very serious. The next day he showed up in my office ready to start the process. Stunned, I gave him the transplant coordinator's contact information and he went on his way. It took about three months to get all the testing and arrangements made for Hayden's transplant. Hayden and the donor did not even meet until a week before the surgery. The transplant was to occur in December, which was of great concern to me because the law student had final exams that month.

First-year law student final exams are unique; they are used as a weed-out tool. Those students who fall below the grade point line are let go. The process used to anger me but I soon realized that schools do it to save students a lot of heartache and debt in the long run. If a student can't hack the first term of law school, things are only going to get worse for them moving forward; racking up additional student loan debt just makes the stress worse. It is better to let them go before they find themselves in a tough spot come bar exam time. I have known too many students who squeak by law school, only to find it impossible to pass the bar.

On December 13, 2004, the law student finished his final exams and the next day, he gave his kidney to my husband.

The surgery went well, and the young man was released from the hospital after two days of observation. He recouped at our house for another day before driving home to Kentucky to be with his family.

Thinking about that young man's sacrifice still gives me chills today. He literally saved my husband's life. What a miracle!

God's Planned Outcome

I was accustomed to controlling most situations. Given my past, I was very proactive when trouble hit. I would spring into action, worry and make myself sick with anxiety, but eventually resolve the problem. I learned to become self-reliant. I did not need anyone. God had another plan. God sent me a 21-year-old donor, who turned out to be a perfect candidate for the transplant. A young, strong, athlete with a selfless heart. Through this young man, God taught me compassion, kindness and community. God also revealed the importance of trusting Him, not myself. He is in control, not me.

God's Holy Word

Do not be anxious about anything, but in everything by prayer and supplication with thanksgiving let your requests be made known to God. (Philippians 4:6 ESV)

Blessed is the man who trusts in the Lord, whose trust is the Lord. He is like a tree planted by water, that sends out its roots by the stream, and does not fear when heat comes, for its leaves remain green, and is not anxious in the year of drought, for it does not cease to bear fruit. (Jeremiah 17:7-8 ESV)

Commit your way to the Lord; trust in him, and he will act.
(Psalm 37:5 ESV)

Questions to Reflect On

1. How many times have you tried to control a situation?
2. What do you do when things don't turn out as planned? How do you cope?
3. What will you do now that I shared this story? Will you try to do a better job of trusting God with your future situations?

II

BEAUTIFUL

RELATIONSHIP WITH GOD

Beautiful begins with a relationship with God! Fast-forward 15 years since my husband's kidney transplant, and I can attest that God has steadily been working in my life. Don't get me wrong, I still face challenges, but now when I face those times of trial, I have a different mindset. I can still have joy despite my circumstances. Why? Because I have developed a strong relationship with God who knows the plan. Not just any plan, the plan He designed specifically for me. The plan confirms He loves me and wants only good things for me.

It took me a long time to realize that accepting God was merely a first step. To really experience God, you need to have a relationship with Him. You need to have the desire to want a relationship and then you need to seek Him out.

He is our Father and knows everything, but still wants to

hear from us. We are His children. He wants us to share our thoughts and feelings with Him. Sharing means we not only bring requests during the bad times, but we also bring praises during the good times! He wants us to include him in every-thing we do in our daily lives, in our work, in our families…in everything.

At first, learning to have a relationship with God was a bit foreign. I had never been taught how to do so. I learned through Sunday Sermons, community with others at church, and most importantly, through his Holy Word.

God reaches us in so many ways. He tells us if we seek Him, we will find Him. He also tells us that nothing will sepa-rate us from His love. To build a relationship with Him, you may initially struggle as I did, but pray earnestly for Him to lead the way and He will guide you. He will reveal Himself to you in the way that is meant just for you.

When you build a relationship with God there is no denying His presence in your life. A relationship does not mean you live a life without heartache or pain, but it does mean you are never alone. I love my relationship with God and how He finds me every day.

My day typically starts with a letter to God, thanking him for every blessing that comes to mind. A good night of rest, another day of life, beautiful weather, a wonderful family, and His pres-ence. Always His presence. I tell Him what is on my heart in that moment and I pray for His guidance in whatever situation I bring to Him. Then I wait. Sometimes God responds immediately through my morning devotion with an exact response via Scripture, and other times I wait and wait, and wait some more.

Over the years, I have learned that waiting is not bad, provided I continue to trust Him while I wait. Early on in my relationship with God, I would grow impatient, which caused me to make poor choices in my quest to control things. But we don't have the plans for our future, God does, so trying to control a situation doesn't always end up the same way it should, especially if we would just hold fast to God's promises.

God promises us answers and blessings but not necessarily on this side of Heaven. For instance, in sharing my story of the loss of my daughter, Camryn, I did not mention that through that time of sorrow, I prayed continually for her to be healed. When she died, I thought that God did not hear me. It took me a long time to realize that God heard me and he healed Camryn; she is healed in Heaven. She does not suffer from any ailments and doesn't feel any pain from the condition that afflicted her earthly body. She is beautiful and perfect, just as God intended her to be.

A relationship with God is a game changer. He transforms how you look at everything. You see with your spiritual eyes, not just your flawed human eyes. With your spiritual eyes, everything seems possible. You no longer worry about things you can't control. You are no longer anxious over every issue, and you know exactly where to turn should any of those old feelings return.

You also gain confidence in your ability to stand strong against the enemy. His lies and attacks do not impact you any longer because you know he has already been conquered through our victory in Christ.

The fear I used to have for God when I was a child and young adult has changed. The fear has changed to reverence. He is worthy to be praised and respected. Now I fear not having a relationship with him. I never want to be the one lost sheep again. I never want to walk alone trying to manage my own life. It is lonely being separated from the one who created you.

God's Planned Outcome

God sought me out. Every trial I encountered drew me little by little closer to him. I learned to become dependent on Him instead of myself, which is His plan for all of us. He does not want us to suffer. He does not want us to be alone. He tells us that seeking approval from man does not bode well for us. A relationship with Him is what is required. For that reason, He has placed a void in our hearts that only He can fill.

God's Holy Word

For am I now seeking the approval of man, or of God? Or am I trying to please man? If I were still trying to please man, I would not be a servant of Christ. (Galatians 1:10 ESV)

He has made everything beautiful in its time. Also, he has put eternity into man's heart, yet so that he cannot find out what God has done from the beginning to the end. (Ecclesiastes 3:11 ESV)

We love because he first loved us. (1 John 4:19 NIV)
I love those who love me, and those who seek me find me. (Proverbs 8:17 NIV)

For God so loved the world that he gave his one and only Son, that whoever believes in him shall not perish but have eternal life. (John 3:16 NIV)

Questions to Reflect On

1. How strong is your relationship with God? Would you like it to be stronger?
2. What would it take on your part to builder a strong relationship with him?
3. Does reading the scripture shared make you feel loved by God?

RESTORATION

It finally clicked God loves me. I do not need to fear Him; I need to seek Him and draw close to Him.

He loves you too!

The early part of my testimony was filled with so much tragedy and pain, but that was not the entire story. The other part of my testimony contains blessing after blessing and my story is still not over. Every day I feel the Lord's presence and know that He is working in my life. Can you feel Him too?

Hold on to your seat because you are going to be blown away by the incredible restoration that can only come from God!

Blessings

As you know, my husband, Hayden, received a transplanted kidney 15 years ago from a stranger, but what I did not share is that the young man became one of his closest friends. He is part of our family and forever will be.

Our son who was born during that time of trial is healthy and 15-years-old now. He excels in school and has a special relationship with my husband. Their bond grew strong when my husband was able to care for him as a stay-at-home dad for the first 7 months of his life.

Remember my daughters? They are all grown up and in their 30s with kids of their own. Yes, I am a grandma of six. One grandson, four granddaughters and one grand-baby on the way. What an incredible legacy God has given me. I went from losing my family all at once to having a family that God continues to multiply.

My mom was released from prison after serving seven years of her sentence. She lived with me for a while, but our relationship was not perfect. After 15 years of ups and downs in our relationship, I gave in. God taught me to have compassion, to love unconditionally as He does. That love gave me courage to help. The outpouring of love was so great that, I believe it broke through the walls that my mother had built for so many years. She finally got it: God loved her and I loved her. I think she learned to let go and how to love, too.

Today, my mother is a Christian, a college graduate, and one of my best friends. I never thought that I would see the day when my mother would be transformed. Given our rocky start and everything we endured, I certainly didn't think we would be close. Today we have an unspoken competition of who can demonstrate more love by surprising each other with heartfelt cards of encouragement. It is so fun. She tells me all the time how proud she is of me and how I am the best thing she ever did with her life. I would say that the best thing she ever did was to accept Jesus into heart (and then yes, I am the next best thing). Wink, wink mom!

Oh, and remember early in the book I told you that my mother had a daughter that I never knew...when my mom became a Christian, she gave me her blessing to find my sister, along with her name and details to help in the process. Little did my mom know, I am pretty good at research. I found a post on a genealogy site that led me to Facebook of all things. Within a day, at age 43, I tracked down my sister, sent her a notification, and within hours she replied. Once we confirmed that we were indeed sisters, my sister and her husband came to visit me in Virginia. To date they have visited twice. We are very close now. She is so much fun. She looks like a younger version of my mom but has my personality. If you see us together, you would never guess that we didn't meet each other until we were in our 40s. To hear our conversations, you would think we had known each other all our lives.

Today, I am a Ph.D. which is basically an academic doctor, a long way from my shaky beginnings. I love how God's plans unfold, especially since I didn't even start college until I was 26 years old. I went from being a teenage mother to holding a terminal degree in a field that I love.

God continues to open doors in my life. I have worked at places like NASA doing some really awesome things, none of which would have happened if God wasn't with me every step of the way, even when I didn't realize it.

God had a vision for my life before I ever existed. He knew what I would endure and what I would become. My freewill may have taken me down the winding road of life, but His grace, love, and mercy straightened my path and gave me a future filled with His promises and blessings!

Praise be to God always!

God's Planned Outcome

There is nothing in this world that God can't fix. Broken relationships, heartache, pain, suffering…the list goes on. God can restore anything. We may not see it all at once or even on this side of Heaven, but God's promises are true. If we believe and seek Him, He promises to give us the desires of our heart. He has blessed me beyond measure and He will do the same for you.

God's Holy Word

I have said these things to you, that in me you may have

peace. In the world you will have tribulation. But take heart. I have overcome the world. (John 16:33 NIV)

For I, the Lord your God, hold your right hand, it is I who say to you, "Fear not, I am the who helps you." (Isaiah 41:13 NIV)

Casting all your anxieties on him, because he cares for you. (1 Peter 5:7 NIV)

Questions to Reflect On

1. How has God moved in your life?
2. What has God restored in your life that you never thought could be fixed?
3. Does learning about the blessings from all my brokenness give you hope that if God can be here for me, He can be there for you, too?

GOD'S VISION TO MY PURPOSE

God had a vision for me; He knit me in my mother's womb and gave me a purpose. All the brokenness experienced brought me to this point in life where I can now help others.

There are times when I thought healing was not possible or a future without pain would exist, but God restores us. It may not be right away, but it happens. It took me a long time to realize that we are the ones who need the extra time, not God. Time is merely a blink of an eye to him.

God didn't need the extra time to work on me; I needed the time to grow my courage stronger. I continue to share God has a purpose for our lives--for us to rise to our calling--but to get there, He must equip us.

Looking back, it is His strength that gave me the will to persevere through every trial and tribulation. Once I stopped trying to control every situation and learned to trust Him in all areas, things changed. I gained a relationship with Him. I received guidance and instruction. I learned a new way forward.

God captured my heart because He never once stopped loving me. Looking back, even when I didn't know why things were happening, He did. He knew where He was taking me and allowed me to experience trials and challenges to get me where I am needed most today.

Without the many trials of life that I dealt with over the years, I would not be able to help others the way God intends for me to do so. I have come to realize that sometimes you need to experience brokenness so that you know what it is to be whole. I experienced brokenness in so many areas. I was a lonely child, I experienced domestic violence, I witnessed tragedy on more than one occasion, I suffered through loss, and I endured great heartbreak.

In every experience, God equipped me a little more. He armed me with full knowledge of what it feels like to experience each circumstance. He put individuals in my life who would help me understand how to deal with those experiences and then he educated me so that I would know how to use everything he taught me along the way to help others.

As I have mentioned several times, God is not surprised by anything. There is nothing you or I could do to that would be an astonishment to Him. There is also nothing that we could break that He can't fix. We can make mistake after mistake, but He has a plan. He has a vision and a purpose for all of us.

Today I own a Christian business called Vision to Purpose, where I serve as a career coach and life coach. My calling (or as the secular world says today, my "why") is to be a light for others so that they can find their way.

There is nothing that will keep God's plans from coming to fruition. I hope my testimony has demonstrated that clearly. Even if you do not have a strong relationship with God yet, He loves you unconditionally and is still working on your behalf. You are your only stumbling block to the goodness God has waiting for you.

God's Planned Outcome

Even before you were born, God thought about you. How exciting is that! You were planned, meant to be. I am always excited by that awesome fact. Even more exciting is that there is nothing you or I can do to change it. God doesn't change His mind. He doesn't waffle on His decisions. He loved us so much that He created us in His own image. Yes, He loved us and gave us an identity, then formed us and gave us a purpose. Praise be to God for His unconditional love. Thank you, Father God!

God's Holy Word

For you formed my inward parts; you knitted me together in my mother's womb. I praise you, for I am fearfully and wonderfully made. Wonderful are your works; my soul knows it very well. My frame was not hidden from you, when I was being made in secret, intricately woven in the depths of the earth. Your eyes saw my unformed substance; in your book were written, every one of them, the days that were formed for me, when as yet there was none of them. Psalm 139: 13-16 ESV)

Questions to Reflect On

1. Can you see what God's vision and purpose is for your life?
2. If you are struggling to see the plans God has for you, what can you do to draw closer to him so you can see?
3. How does knowing God has a plan for you change your outlook on your future?

ACKNOWLEDGMENTS

The idea for this book came years ago when friends and family suggested I tell my story. Time after time I would get the "you should write a book" statement. At the time I thought they were just being nice. After all they were my friends and family, isn't that what they are supposed to say?

I love writing and deep down I always thought sharing my story would happen but every time I sat down to try, I lost steam. Writing about my life always brought about emotions I wasn't ready to deal with until now.

This book is an example of God's plan and His perfect timing. To help me move forward, He put all the right people in my path like my husband, Hayden, who has always supported my endeavors. I love you and thank you for always letting me be me, even if you do not always understand my crazy thoughts.

And, for my children Sandra, Brittany and Zachary who taught me how to be fearless and appreciate life. They are my pride and joy!

To my mom, Pam who is my rock and my mother-in-law, Beverly who continues to teach me how to have fun.

God also connected me with Christy Barritt, who is an amazing author of more than 70 books. She has been such an encouragement and wealth of knowledge throughout this entire process. Thank you, Christy, for being my friend and a shining light. I am forever grateful!

He brought Mark Lambertson, a former colleague and amazing graphic designer back into my life. Mark not only designed my logo but also the cover for this book. Thank you, Mark, for your friendship and creative talent.

He kept me connected to a former colleague who has been a constant source of encouragement. Thank you, Lisa Marie, for being my friend/editor and for helping my words make sense to others. And, yes, for the serial comma! I am so blessed to have you in my life!

And to all those friends God put in my life who have been with me through some of my most challenging moments: Sue, Lareina, and Marietta. You are my sisters and I love you.

Thank you to the ladies in the Women's Group at Kempsville Christian Church. I love learning about God with all of you!

A special thank you to the ladies in the Women's Group at Avalon Church of Christ who allowed me to share my story during their mini retreat! I was so blessed by your support and encouragement as I shared with the group. You gave me courage to write this book.

Most of all, I am thankful to God for His grace, love and mercy. Thank you, God for loving me and never leaving me. Thank you for giving me life and a purpose!

FAVORITE SCRIPTURE VERSES

Introduction

There is no one like the God of Jeshurun, who rides on the heavens to help you and on the clouds in his majesty. The eternal God is your refuge, and underneath are the everlasting arms. (Deuteronomy 33:26-27 NIV)

I have said these things to you, that in me you may have peace. In the world you will have tribulation. But take heart; I have overcome the world. (John 16:33 ESV)

And we know that in all things God works for the good of those who love him, who have been called according to his purpose. (Romans 8:28 ESV)

Chapter 1

For you formed my inward parts; you knitted me together in my mother's womb. (Jeremiah 139:13 ESV)

"For I know the plans I have for you", declares the Lord, "plans to prosper you and not to harm you, plans to give you a hope and a future." (Jeremiah 29:11 ESV)

Chapter 2

Whoever heeds instruction is on the path to life, but he who rejects reproof leads others astray. (Proverbs 10:17 ESV)

Offer to God a sacrifice of thanksgiving, and perform your vows to the Most High, and call upon me in the day of trouble; I will deliver you, and you shall glorify me. (Psalms 50:14-15 ESV)

Consider it pure joy, my brothers and sisters, a whenever you face trials of many kinds, because you know that the testing of your faith produces perseverance. Let perseverance finish its work so that you may be mature and complete, not lacking anything. If any of you lacks wisdom, you should ask God, who gives generously to all without finding fault, and it will be given to you. (James 1:2-5 NIV)

Chapter 3

But each person is tempted when he is lured and enticed by his own desire. Then desire when it has conceived gives birth to sin, and sin when it is fully grown brings forth death. (James 1:14-15 ESV)

Finally, brothers, whatever is true, whatever is honorable, whatever is just, whatever is pure, whatever is lovely, whatever is commendable, if there is any excellence, if there is anything worthy of praise, think about these things. (Philippians 4:8 ESV)

And whatever you do, in word or deed, do everything in the name of the Lord Jesus, giving thanks to God the Father through him. (Colossians 3:17 ESV)

Chapter 4

Yet you do not know what tomorrow will bring. What is your life? For you are a mist that appears for a little time and then vanishes. (James 4:4 ESV)

So teach us to number our days that we may get a heart of wisdom. (Psalm 90:12 ESV)

Let all that you do be done in love. (1 Corinthians 16:14 ESV)

Chapter 5

I am the Lord; that is my name; my glory I give to no other, nor my praise to carved idols. Behold, the former things have come to pass, and new things I now declare; before they spring forth I tell you of them. (Isaiah 42:8-9 ESV)

But I the LORD will speak what I will, and it shall be fulfilled without delay. For in your days, you rebellious people, I will fulfill whatever I say, declares the Sovereign LORD. (Ezekiel 12:25 NIV)

Chapter 6

I have said these things to you, that in me you may have peace. In the world you will have tribulation. But take heart; I have overcome the world. (John 16:33 ESV)

He refreshes my soul. He guides me along the right paths for his name's sake. Even though I walk through the darkest valley, I will fear no evil, for you are with me; your rod and your staff, they comfort me. (Psalm 23:3-4 NIV)

For God so loved the world, that he gave his only Son, that whoever believes in him should not perish but have eternal life. (John 3:16 ESV)

Chapter 7

Blessed is the man who remains steadfast under trial, for when he has stood the test he will receive the crown of life, which God has promised to those who love him. (James 1:12 ESV)

Beloved, do not be surprised at the fiery trial when it comes upon you to test you, as though something strange were happening to you. But rejoice insofar as you share Christ's sufferings, that you may also rejoice and be glad when his glory is revealed. (1 Peter 4:12-13 ESV)

When the righteous cry for help, the Lord hears and delivers them out of all their troubles. The Lord is near to the broken-hearted and saves the crushed in spirit. (Psalm 34:17-18 ESV)

Chapter 8

If you forgive those who sin against you, your heavenly father will also forgive you. (Matthew 6:14 NLT)

Anyone who does not love does not know God, because God is love. (1 John 4:8 ESV)

The Lord is not slow to fulfill his promise as some count slow-ness, but is patient toward you, not wishing that any should perish, but that all should reach repentance. (2 Peter 3:9 ESV)

Above all, keep loving one another earnestly, since love covers a multitude of sins. (1 Peter 4:8 ESV)

Chapter 9

He will tend his flock like a shepherd; he will gather the lambs in his arms; he will carry them in his bosom, and gently lead those that are with young. (Isaiah 4:11 NIV)

So he told them this parable: "What man of you, having a hundred sheep, if he has lost one of them, does not leave the ninety-nine in the open country, and go after the one that is lost, until he finds it? And when he has found it, he lays it on his shoulders, rejoicing. And when he comes home, he calls together his friends and his neighbors, saying to them, 'Rejoice with me, for I have found my sheep that was lost.' Just so, I tell you, there will be more joy in heaven over one sinner who repents than over ninety-nine righteous persons who need no repentance. (Luke 15:3-7 ESV)

Chapter 10

Blessed be the God and Father of our Lord Jesus Christ, the Father of mercies and God of all comfort, who comforts us in all our affliction, so that we may be able to comfort those who are in any affliction, with the comfort with which we ourselves are comforted by God. For as we share abundantly in Christ's sufferings, so through Christ we share abundantly in comfort too. (2 Corinthians 1:3-5 ESV)

He heals the brokenhearted and binds up their wounds. (Psalm 147:3 ESV)

Many are the plans in the mind of a man, but it is the purpose of the Lord that will stand. (Proverbs 19:21 ESV)

Chapter 11

Count it all joy, my brothers, when you meet trials of various kinds, for you know that the testing of your faith produces steadfastness. And let steadfastness have its full effect, that you may be perfect and complete, lacking in nothing. (James 1:2-4 ESV)

Now faith is confidence in what we hope for and assurance about what we do not see. (Hebrews 11:1 NIV)

Rejoice always, pray continually, give thanks in all circumstances; for this is God's will for you in Christ Jesus. (1 Thessalonians 5:16-18 NIV)

Chapter 12

Do not be anxious about anything, but in everything by prayer and supplication with thanksgiving let your requests be made known to God. (Philippians 4:6 ESV)

Blessed is the man who trusts in the Lord, whose trust is the Lord. He is like a tree planted by water, that sends out its roots by the stream, and does not fear when heat comes, for its leaves remain green, and is not anxious in the year of drought, for it does not cease to bear fruit. (Jeremiah 17:7-8 ESV)

Commit your way to the Lord; trust in him, and he will act. (Psalm 37:5 ESV)

Chapter 13

For am I now seeking the approval of man, or of God? Or am I trying to please man? If I were still trying to please man, I would not be a servant of Christ. (Galatians 1:10 ESV)

He has made everything beautiful in its time. Also, he has put eternity into man's heart, yet so that he cannot find out what God has done from the beginning to the end. (Ecclesiastes 3:11 ESV)

We love because he first loved us. (1 John 4:19 NIV)

I love those who love me, and those who seek me find me. (Proverbs 8:17 NIV)

For God so loved the world that he gave his one and only Son, that whoever believes in him shall not perish but have eternal life. (John 3:16 NIV)

Chapter 14

I have said these things to you, that in me you may have peace. In the world you will have tribulation. But take heart. I have overcome the world. (John 16:33 NIV)

For I, the Lord your God, hold your right hand, it is I who say to you, "Fear not, I am the who helps you. (Isaiah 41:13 NIV)

Casting all your anxieties on him, because he cares for you. (1 Peter 5:7 NIV)

Chapter 15

For you formed my inward parts; you knitted me together in my mother's womb. I praise you, for I am fearfully and wonderfully made. Wonderful are your works; my soul knows it very well. My frame was not hidden from you, when I was being made in secret, intricately woven in the depths of the earth. Your eyes saw my unformed substance; in your book were written, every one of them, the days that were formed for me, when as yet there was none of them. (Psalm 139: 13-16 ESV)

ABOUT THE AUTHOR

Jeannine Bennett is a wife to Hayden, mom to four children and grandmother to six grandchildren. Her children are named Sandra, Brittany, Camryn and Zachary. Her grandchildren are Colin, Lilyana, Willow, Savannah, Winter, and Hope. She is the founder and CEO of Vision to Purpose, located in Virginia Beach, Virginia, an adjunct faculty member in the School of Business for Liberty University Online, and an executive coach for The Honor Foundation.

To those who know Jeannine, she is simply a woman who loves Jesus, is devoted to her family and struggles with life's challenges like the rest of us. She is not immune to bad hair days, shrinking clothes (weight gain) or sleepless nights. She loves learning and sharing the knowledge acquired to help others learn too. Her favorite ice cream is a toss up between butter pecan and mint chocolate chip. And, although she has lived in Virginia for more than 30 years, she still calls a water fountain a bubbler. A term she grew up saying in her home-town of Racine, Wisconsin.

ABOUT VISION TO PURPOSE

Vision to Purpose is a Christian organization dedicated to helping individuals and organizations succeed through the offering of tailored career, life and business solutions. Some of the services offered by Vision to Purpose include:

- Career and Life Coaching
- Resume and Cover Letter Writing
- Job Search Strategies and Interview Prep
- Professional Development
- Copy Writing
- Strategic Communications
- Speech Writing
- Public Speaking
- Project Management
- And More…

To learn more about Vision to Purpose, visit: www.visiontopurpose.com.

If you were inspired by Broken to Beautiful and want to continue to receive encouraging messages daily, please connect with us on Facebook at www.facebook.com/Visionto-Purpose/ or follow us on LinkedIn at www.linkedin.com/company/vision-to-purpose/

If you are interested in having Jeannine speak at your church or event, visit www.visiontopurpose.com and click on "contact us."